A
HAND BOOK TO THE JAFFNA PENINSULA

A HAND BOOK TO THE JAFFNA PENINSULA

AND A SOUVENIR OF THE OPENING OF THE RAILWAY TO THE NORTH

S. KATIRESU

GYAN

Published by

Gyan Publishing House
5, Ansari Road
Daryaganj, New Delhi-110002
Phone: 011-47034999, 9811692060
E-mail: books@gyanbooks.com

Distribution Network
gyanbooks.com
India, USA, Canada, UK, Australia, France

ISBN : 978-81-212-3463-4 (PB)
First Published, Jaffna, 1905
Author: S. Katiresu

2nd Impression 2020

Printed at: Gyan Press, Delhi.

A Hand Book to the Jaffna Peninsula
Author: S. Katiresu

A

Hand Book

to the

Jaffna Peninsula

and a

Souvenir of the Opening of the Railway to the North.

by

S. Katiresu,

Proctor, District Court, Jaffna.

Printed at the

American Ceylon Mission Press.

Tellippallai, Jaffna.

1905.

To

The Memory

of the late

C. W. Katiravelpillai, Esquire, C.C.S.

Advocate,

&c.

this Handbook is

respectfully

inscribed

by the Compiler.

PREFACE.

Mr. J. S. Drieberg, Office Asst. to the Government Agent, Western Province, suggested to me the preparation of a Gazetteer of the Jaffna Peninsula which it is believed will be useful to strangers desiring information of the hitherto isolated country to be opened up by the Railway. Accordingly I have prepared this little handbook which is issued to the public on the occssion of the opening of the Railway to through traffic.

My thanks are due to Mr. James H. Martyn, Editor, *Catholic Guardian*, Mr. S. T. Arnold, Proctor and Mr. F. B. Mailvaganam for the kind assistance rendered in the compilation of this book.

My thanks are also due to the Rev. J. H. Dickson for the get up of this book, as well as for several kind suggestions.

This little handbook is presented to the public not only as a Gazetteer of the Jaffna Peninsula, as was suggested by my esteemed friend Mr. Drieberg who was in our midst for a considerable period as a successful and popular Magistrate, but also as a Souvenir of the opening of the Jaffna Railway for which we are deeply indebted to our late Governor, Sir Joseph West Ridgeway, who will be regarded for all time as the greatest benefactor of the Jaffna people.

The Surveyor-General having written to say that he cannot, at the present time, supply me with copies of the map of Jaffna, I am compelled to make use ot the accompanying rough sketch.

Jaffna, S. KATIRESU.

July 21, 1905

PREFACE

Contents.

Chapter I.

GEOGRAPHY.

General. The Jaffna Peninsula is the extreme North of Ceylon, about 9° 40′ North of the Equator and 80° East of Greenwich. It covers an area of about 1,262 square miles, with a population of 300,851 according to the last census taken in 1901. The number of persons per square mile is 238. The figures include Punakari, Karachi and Tunukkai which are outside the Peninsula.

The Peninsula would be an island in itself but for the fact that in the dry season, it is connected with the mainland by a narrow strip of land. At present there are permanent bridges, one for the cart-road and another for the railway. The bridges are at Elephant Pass, about 33 miles from Jaffna Town. Towards the west of the Peninsula is a cluster of small Islands with Portuguese and Dutch names.

Divisions. Ceylon with a population of 3,565,954 is divided into nine Provinces, viz:—Western, Central, Northern, Southern, Eastern, North-Western, North-Central, Uva and Sabaragamuva Provinces. The Northern Province ranks as the third with a population of 340,936, the first two being Western (920,683) and Central (622,832).

The Northern Province is again divided into the following divisions, viz:—

Jaffna Division (with a population of 45,679),
Valikamam East (24,403),
Valikamam North (44,401),
Valikamam West (45,860),
Vadamirachchi East (4,247),
Vadamirachchi West (48,548),
Tenmirachchi (37,648),
Pachchilaippalai (6,076),
Delft (3,906),
The Islands (32,656),
Punakari (4,817),
Karaichchi (2,879) and
Tunukkai (638).

The Divisions of Punakari. Karaichchi and Tunukkai being outside the Peninsula, are not taken notice of in this handbook.

The Peninsula is flat and very low being only 9 feet above sea level. It is indented by shallow lagoons. The highest point Keerimalai some 40 ft. above sea level is about two miles west of the Kangesanturai Railway Station. Keerimalai has become a fashionable health resort to large numbers throughout Ceylon and even South India and to the springs in the vicinity (covered by the sea at high tide) they resort for their baths.

The Roads are broad and regular, generally neat-looking and white. It is the opinion of many a traveller that they compare well with the best roads of the world. They are pronounced first class by ardent admirers of the wheel. "Jaffna is perhaps the only part of Ceylon in which the native population seem clearly to appreciate the value of roads, and are anxious to afford every facility and contribute every assistance for their construction" Tennent.

The Climate is hot and dry with but little moisture in the atmosphere. The mean temperature is 81°. 2′. This is the highest mean for the whole of Ceylon; but the maximum has been reached at Trincomalie at 103.7° in May 1890. The highest for Jaffna was 101.6° in April 1896. The average rainfall is 45.09 inches for the year being only next to the lowest which is 38·34 inches for Mannar. The longest drought had in Jaffna was for 137 days from May to September in 1884. This would be the highest if not for Mannar which heads the list with ·159 days from April to September 1887.

Two Monsoons (the Arabic term *mansim*-a season) or seasonal winds prevail. The north-east monsoon blows from November to February bringing rain. The south-west monsoon begins in April and lasts till September. The month of March is close and intensely hot. The change of temperature is never sudden.

The Divisions of Vadamirachi and Valigamam North are considered the most healthy, the death rate being from 15 to 20 per 1,000.

Soil. Coral rocks abound from above sea level and extend across the Peninsula where the land has been "generally upraised from the Eastern to the Western shore." Sand covers a vast extent of the Peninsula. The palmyrah and cocoanut trees grow freely on it.

The arable soil is generally of a dark and red colour, from the admixture of iron and being largely composed of lime from the comminuted coral: it is susceptible of successful cultivation and produces fairly good crops more due to the industry of the people than to the soil. The soil is responsive to systematic cultivation, but is imperfectly adapted for maturing a constant succession of seeds and cereal productions.

For towns and villages see later chapters.

Chapter II.

EARLY HISTORY.

Origin of Jaffna. A certain Kaviveerarakavan from South India, an expert in vocal music and one skilled in the use of the instrument called the *Yal* so delighted the king NarasinghaRaja of Ceylon that he was pleased to present him with the Jaffna Peninsula then a *Manatidal* (literally sandy plain). The Singer was called *Yalpady* and his land *Yalpanam*. This name is even now retained in Tamil and the foreign settlers and rulers have either corrupted or improved it into *Jaffna.* The colloquial form of *Yalpanam* is *Yappanam.* Now the sounds of *Ya* and *Ja* are easily interchangeable. So are those of *pp* and *ff.* Thus *Yappanam* is easily interchangeable into *Jaffanam.* As soon as it went into a foreign language it lost the Tamil ending *m.* Consequently it stood as *Jaffana.* As the result of the natural inclination to make a name short and sweet the second *a* was dropped. Thus we have the present name *Jaffna*, the original *Yalpanam* being still retained in Tamil.

The *Yalpady* to make the best use of his land brought his own men from India who in time became settlers gradually spreading over the land. On his death they were ill treated by the Singhalese intruders and invaders. King KoolanghaiSinghaiaryan hearing of this came from South India and released such of the sufferers as chose to remain.

Tamil Kings. Circa 104 A. D. Koolanghai built a palace and a flower garden at Nallore (within the gravets of the present Jaffna Town), and became the first ruling king resident at Jaffna. During his peaceful reign some *Vellales* came from South India and settled in the villages of Tinnevely, Mailiddy, Tellipalai, Inuvil, Tolpuram, Irupalai. Koilakandy, Puloly and Pachchilaipaly and in the Island of Delft.

He is said to have brought water from the *Jumna* river and put it in a well then sunk for the purpose and now called Jumnary and situated next to the C. M. S. Church at Nallore. He built four temples: Veyiluvantha-PillaiarKovil to the East of the palace, Chaddanatha-Kovil to the North, VeeramakaliammanKovil to the West and KailayaPillaiarKovil to the South. The ruins of the palace are still to be seen. The temples were destroyed by the Portuguese. New temples with the original names have now risen on the old sites.

The first founder of the kingly dynasty died leaving behind his son KulasekaraSinghaiaryan, who was soon followed by his son KulathungaSinghaiaryan. He greatly encouraged agriculture in Jaffna.

WickramaSinghaiaryan the successor and son of Kulathunga distinguished himself by quelling a fight between the Singhalese and Tamils of the Kingdom. His son VarotheyaSinghaiaryan's reign was uneventful.

His son MarthandaSinghaiaryan is remembered for the measures he adopted for the higher education of his subjects and for the improvement he effected in cultivation. He lived a very humble aud examplary life.

GoonapooshanaSinghaiaryan his son and successor walked in the footsteps of his father in being very humble and in encouraging trade and education. He was followed by his son VarothoyaSinghaiaryan who was more valiant than any of his predecessors. The

Wannias incited the Singhalese to rise in rebellion against him. He put down the Singhalese and duly punished the Wannias. His help was asked for by SanthirasekaraPandian, king of Madura to drive the foreigners from their kingdom. Varotheya helped him successfully and returned to Jaffna. His end was sudden and suspicion hovers over it even to the present day.

SeyaveeraSinghaiaryan the valiant son of a valiant father fought the Kandyan king Poovanakavago over the rights to the pearl fishery. Seyaveera being the victor became the ruler of all Ceylon. Later on the Kandyan king was allowed to rule his provinces on his consenting to pay an annual tribute.

The next Tamil king was GoonaveeraSinghaiaryan, the son of Seyaveera. In this reign the tribute being delayed by the Kandyan king, some tracts of land were wrested from him. He like his grandfather was of some use to the then Madura King

Then came the troubles with the new king KanagasooriaSinghaiaryan, son of Goonaveera. He lost the kingdom and the Kandyan king Vijayavagu reigned over Jaffna for 17 years.

Kanagasooria and his two sons brought an army from India and drove out the Singhalese kings. The father entrusted the kingdom into the hands of Singhapararajasekaram, the elder son and led a quiet and retired life. The new king had two wives and one concubine. He had Singhavago and Pandaram by one wife, Paranirupasingham by the other and Sangily by the concubine. The king's brother Sekarajasekaram brought *Pundits* from India and established a "*Sangam*" (an Academy). Many literary works were undertaken. He was the author of Raguvamsam, Sekarajasekaram and other standard works.

Singhavago having died in his young age the king put his second son Pandaram on the throne and went on a pilgrimage to India with Sangily. Sangily was a very mischievous lad. For some disturbance or other created by him, he and his father were thrown into prison by the Chola King. Paranirupasingham heard of their distress and had them released. The king on his return rewarded Paranirupasingham for his good services by giving him seven villages viz: Kalliamkadu, Achchuvely, Udupitty, Mallakam, Chandilippay, Araly and Kachchai. He was also to have precedence over all others except Pandaram.

Sangily was very jealous of the precedence given to Paranirupasingham. So taking the opportunity of Paranirupasingham's absence in India, he assasinated Pandaram the king and usurped the throne. Paranirupasingham, not being able to do aught against the usurper became his minister. His control over the seven villages passed into the hands of the usurper. This state of things was not pleasing to the minister and consequently he conspired against the king. He began by writing a letter to Kakkai Wannia at Kaits asking him to bring the Portuguese from India and promising that he would render them every help to wrest the kingdom from Sangily.

Portuguese days, 1617 to 1658 A. D. Soon after some Portuguese styling themselves traders came to Jaffna and landed at Pannaiturai (behind the present fort).

They applied to Sangily for permission to trade in Jaffna. The minister tried to persuade the unwilling king to give permission and with some difficulty the king allowed them to trade by day and return to their vessels in the nights. Shortly after the wily Portuguese brought valuable presents to the king who was so taken up by them that he allowed the Portuguese to have a residence outside the then town. The Portuguese in the thick of the jungle and in secret built a mud fortress and collected a lot of arms and ammunition. One day when the king was on his way returning from hunting, he saw the fortress and ordered it to be destroyed. The Portuguese objected to this and offered resistance. For seven days the fight went on and the Portuguese with their antequated fire arms were defeated by an army which knew not of the use of them. The fortress was destroyed.

The remaining Portuguese went to Kakkai Wannia at Kaits and threatened to kill him because he had not helped them in the fight. In the meantime the minister who was so very sorry had written to the Wannia that he could help the Portuguese in another attempt. They took the hint and with the help of a fresh contingent of men and a supply of ammunition made the second attempt. The Wannia in the act of saluting caught hold of the king and would not let go his hold. Thereupon the minister ordered that the army should take no arms without the order of the commander-in-chief (i. e. the King). Thus the Portuguese got all they wanted and in 1617 A. D. their flag was hoisted in Jaffna they having come to Ceylon in 1505 A. D.

In 1622 the Tamils, to use Tennent's words, true to their hereditary instinct, again attempted to come in but failed.

The king Sangily, after a farcical trial, was put to the sword. The queen who heard of his death killed herself. The children were sent to Tranquebar which was a Portuguese territory. The "good" Paranirupasingham got his 7 villages back with Nallore and Mathakal in addition. He was the minister of the Portuguese as well.

A prize of 25,000 rix-dollars* was offerred to the person who brought Pararajasekara. A brahmin who knew of his whereabouts went up to him and availed himself of a suitable opportunity to sever his head with a sword. He brought it to the Portuguese who gave the scoundrel his due by cutting his head off saying that they wanted Pararajasekara himself and not his head.

The policy of the Portuguese was governed by territorial ambition, commercial greed and religious proselytism. This policy was prosecuted with bigotry and cruelty which would be incredible if there were not the testimony of their own historians. The Roman Catholic form of Christianity was forced on the people. All the temples were destroyed except those at Nallore and Keerimalai which were reserved for the same fate on the death of Paranirupasingham. In the ninth year of the Portuguese reign he died and his son Pararajasingham† who was given the title of *Madapaly* and *Muthaly* succeeded his father.

During this short stay of forty years of the Portuguese reign, some *Vellales* from Karaikal settled at Karative and Vaddukkoddai. A certain Ulagunalamuthaly from the Chola country also came to Kalapoomy in Karative.

Dutch rule 1658 to 1795 A. D. Jaffna surrendered to the Dutch after a seige of 3½ months on the 22nd, June,

* This coin, current even under British rule, was worth 75 cents and was called "*Rasal*" in Tamil.

† Pararajasingham had seven sons and one daughter among whom he divided his possessions as follows: to Alakanmaivallamuthaly, Nallore and Kalliamkado; to Thanapalasinghamuthaly, Mallakam; to Vettivalauthamuthaly, Sandilippay; to Vijeyatheivanthiramuthaly, Araly; to Idaveerasinghamuthaly, Achchuvely; to Santhirasekaramappanamuthaly, Uduppitty; to Rajandiramuthaly, Kachehai and to his daughter Vethavally who was married among the Vellales, Mathakal.

1658. Fort Hammenheil at the entrance to the Kaits harbour had fallen to them on the 10th April, 1658.

Reformed Dutch Christianity was introduced into Jaffna by Rev. Dr. Baldeus in August 1658. Proclamation was then issued forbidding the harbouring or concealing of Roman Catholic priests under pain of death.

In 1736 A. D. a press for printing books in the native language was established in Colombo by the Dutch Government. In 1749 the New Testament was translated from Greek into Tamil by the Rev. Philip Melho a clergyman at Jaffna.

In 1785 paper currency was introduced into Ceylon, but it was left to Sir Arthur Gordon a century afterwards to introduce Government notes thus extending an cfficial guarantee and removing the distrust of people for Bank notes.

The policy of the Dutch was far more progressive and peaceful, though, as regards commerce, their policy was selfish and oppressive. They developed cultivation and improved the means of communication especially by canals. The education of the people occupied a good deal of official attention, as also their Christianization through a staff of Dutch chaplains; the system of employing only Protestant Christians created many a hypocrite.

They had their head quarters at Colombo. The Governor in Jaffna had two *Mudaliyars* by the names of Anthirasy and Poothatamby. An untoward incident in their families has been the subject of a drama.

Anthirasy being taken by the beauty of Poothatamby's wife sent word to her to pay him a private visit. In reply the lady sent a broomstick and an old pair of slippers which made Anthirasy very indignant. He waited for an opportunity to revenge this insult. He, as co-*Mudaliyar*, asked Poothatamby to sign a blank paper which he did in a weak moment. Then Anthirasy wrote out a letter on this blank paper offering help to the Portuguese. Anthirasy was in high favour with the Governor and brought about a trial by night (which was against the rule) and had Poothatamby sentenced to death. Before any appeal could be made against the hasty sentence to the authorities in Colombo poor Poothatamby was put to death. The Governor and Anthirasy however were at length summoned to Colombo. Anthirasy who went by land was killed by an elephant and the Governor who went by sea threw himself overboard.

British regime from 1795. In September 1795 A. D. the British took the reins of Government to our great advantage. Ceylon was first under the Governor of Madras and in 1802 it was declared a Crown Colony under a separate Governor—Hon. F. North being the first chosen. A passing notice of the more notable events under British rule may not be out of place.

Freedom of religion and liberty of speech which were denied under the two previous Governments were guaranteed to all the people of Ceylon of whatever race or creed in 1805.

The system of trial by jury, a privilege greatly prized by Englishmen, was introduced into the Island in 1811.

It was not till 1844 that slavery, perhaps the greatest curse under the previous governments, was finally abolished.

The bandages round the fisherman and the paddy cultivator that pressed so hard on them were removed, the former in 1840 and the latter in 1892, when respectively they were declared free to breathe, the one refreshing ozone of the seas and the other zephyrs laden with the fragrance of the fields.

Courts of Requests for the settlement of small civil disputes and claims were established in 1845.

The Police force was introduced into Jaffna in the year 1866, and two years after, the Ceylon Rifles were disbanded as the result of which the garrison in the fort was removed.

The telegraph was introduced into Jaffna in 1869 and since then small extensions have been made to Manippay, Kankesanturai, Valvettyturai and Pt. Pedro.

The Peninsula is now fully opened up by excellent roads constructed under the direction of Major Skinner, Mr. Dyke and their successors.

Education in Jaffna, has been chiefly due to Missionary enterprise, which, since the year 1870 when the Department of Public Instruction was introduced by Sir Hercules Robinson, has been greatly aided by grants given on the result-payment system. The people are amply provided with the means of education in which they have taken precedence over many other parts of the Island.

Chapter III.

RACES AND CREED.

Races.* The chief races within the Peninsula are the Tamils, Moors, Burghers, Europeans and Americans; but it is the Tamils who form the overwhelming majority of the population.

The Tamils are the foremost of the Dravidian races who in the dim and distant past prior even to the Aryan conquest colonized India. And even though they subsequently came under the domination of Aryan civilization they have with singular persistance retained their individuality even to this day.

The Dravidian race, says the reporter on the Census of 1901, "appeared in India before the Aryan or the Dasyus, whom they subdued, and belong to a stock which is sometimes called the Ural-Attaic, Scythian, or Turanian family, and which was widely distributed. It founded the ancient civilization of Babylonia, and colonized long before the Aryans. Among its descendants are the Lapps and Finns of Northern Europe, the Basques of the Pyrennees, the Magyars of Hungary, the Ottaman Turks, the Ostiaks and other Ugrians of Siberia. Linquistic and other affinities seems to indicate that the inhabitants of some

* From the valuable report on Census of 1901 we gather the following figures shewing the number of each of the several races in the Peninsula, Europeans 110, Burghers 476, Singhalese 226, Moors 3078, Malays 60, Tamils 296,805 and others 306. These figures include Punnakari, Tunukkai and Karachchi. Total 300,851.

of the Islands of the Pacific ocean and the aboriginal tribes of South and West Australia were derived from Dravidian settlements in India or from an earlier common source. The Dravidians probably once occupied the greater part of Northern India, where traces of their blood and speech are still found, but their seat from the dawn of history has been South India. They are also called the Tamilian race, because the Tamils are the oldest and most influential representatives of the race."

"The Ceylon Tamils," says the same writer, "are the descendants of the bands of Tamils who came over upon the invitation of the first Singhalese King Wijaya and his successors to develop the country; and of later bands, by whom Ceylon was frequently overrun, and who on several occassions acquired the supreme power. The indigenous Tamils inhabit for the most part the Northern and Eastern Provinces. The Jaffna District which is the chief centre of the population is (says Sir Emerson Tennent), 'almost the only place in Ceylon, of which it might be said that no one is idle or unprofitably employed. . . . There is a satisfaction experienced in no other part of Ceylon in visiting their villages and farms and in witnessing the industrious habits and improved processes of the peasantry'."

It is however difficult to understand why Sir Emerson Tennent should conclude his estimate of the Jaffna Tamils with the unmerited observation, that "the same energy of character in which the Tamils of Jaffna constitutionally excel the Singhalese and Kandyans, which is strikingly exhibited in all their ordinary pursuits is equally perceptible in its *vicious* as in its moral development." Without giving any instances whatever he referred to the social arrangements of the higher classes saying that "when these can be examined" they "exhibit a picture of demoralisation truly deplorable." If he had but paused to consider the moral degradation of the "Society" of West End, it is hardly likely that he would have come to this *truly deplorable* conclusion.

Speaking of the lowest classes he says that "their practices are *inconceivably vile.*" He gives instances of cases of sorcery and witchcraft, one of which he says was officially brought under his notice in 1849. He refers again to a case of witchcraft brought under the notice of the Police Court in 1848. The case, he says, went to its legitimate end and he laments over the result that the accused was acquitted. Had the Police Magistrate even then to answer queries from the Colonial Secretary?

Possibly the reader should be as indulgent to Tennent for making these unjust observations as for his making mention of a palmyrah oil* which is unknown and unheard of in this country.

"All throughout Ceylon," says Bishop Caldwell, "the coolies in the coffee plantations are Tamilians, the majority of the money-making classes even in Colombo are Tamilians. . . Tamil is the prevailing language in all the military cantonments in Southern India, whatever be the vernacular language of the district. The majority of the Klings (Kalingas) or Hindus who are found in the further east are Tamilans, a large proportion of the coolies who have emigrated in such numbers to the Mauritius and to the West Indian Colonies are Tamilians. In short, wherever money is to be made, wherever a more apathetic or a more aristocratic people is waiting to be pushed aside, thither swarm the Tamilians—the Greeks

* See Tennent vol. 1 p. 111.

or Scotch of the East, the least superstitious and the most enterprising, and persevering race of Hindus."

"The emigration," says Mr. Ievers, "of young men to the Straits, Burmah and other places in search of employment continues to be on the increase. The Jaffnese are a singularly industrious and economical race, and seldom fail to save some money, however poor their income may be. They are very thrifty; and this striking feature in their character prevents them from falling into that squalid poverty which is the condition of the lower classes in other parts of the Island."

When we consider how little of this sandy waste is left uncultivated and to what perfection without the aid of school-taught science agriculture has been brought in this country, and with what industry an arid waste has been covered with a perennial green in the absence of tanks and rivers, we need not wonder that even the most casual travellers have borne such glowing testimony to the perseverence and industry of the Jaffna Tamil.

The Tamils are besides a thrifty, law abiding, shrewd, intelligent, educated and grateful people. Successive Government Agents and Chief Justices have with satisfaction noted the comparative absence of serious crimes* in the district.

The Naddukoddai Chetties are also Tamils but not Jaffnese. They are "men from the Indian Coast with shaved heads and the scantiest of clothing, dealers chiefly in rice, cloth and money,- 'cute gentlemen who only ask up to 60 per cent for accomodation and take good care in advancing the principal to deduct the interest."

---

* For the whole of Ceylon there are only 92 Jaffnese in jail—Report on census 1901.

The Chetties are first rate accountants, but to this day keep all their accounts on ola books. Many of them are reputed to be very wealthy. It was at one time considered among the mercantile community that a Chetty's word was as good as a bond, but of late years they have had huge law suits, and the high position once occupied by them has been somewhat undermined.

The Moors. Mr. P. Arunachalem writes:* "According to its strict interpretation, the term 'Moor' which means an inhabitant of Morocco, is misleading when applied to the people of Ceylon who go by that name, and who do not lay claim to an African origin. In Ceylon the term is a relic of the rule of the Portuguese, who gave to the Ceylon Mohammedan the name of his co-religonist of Morocco, and is used to designate all Mohammedans (other than Malays) born in Ceylon or southern India and speaking Tamil as their mother tongue."

The Moors of Jaffna are the descendants of one Snatha Saibo and his friends who came from Kailpatnam (East of Cape Comorin) and settled at Meerusuvil South for purposes of trade. They called South Meerusuvil, 'Usan'. From there they came over to Nallore whence they were driven by the Tamils by throwing pigs into their wells as it was considered that the proximity of the Islamites to the sacred shrine was improper. The Moors sold their lands and went to *Navaiturai,* now called Navanturai. They are a race of shop-keepers and petty traders, while a handful of them have settled down as agriculturists.

Other races. Among the other races the most important are the European and the American. Of the

---

* See the Report on the Census 1901. vol. i. p. 81.

former those who have to do with the Peninsula are chiefly civil servants and Missionaries with a handful of planters. The Missionaries belong to the Anglican, Congregational, Weslyan and Roman Catholic communions. Of the latter all who have arrived since the year 1816 have been engaged exclusively in Missionary work.

Religion.*

Most of Jaffnese are Hindus, a good number of them are Roman Catholics and a fair number are Protestants. We find a great deal of friendly feeling among the followers of the several religions. Let us hope that the spirit of tolerance so characteristic of our race will, with the advance of culture, be fostered.

* From the valuable report on the Census of 1901 we gather the following figures shewing the number of each of the several religionists in the Peninsula. Hindus 265,875, Mohammedans 3,085, Roman Catholics 26,804, Church of England Christians including those of the C. M. S. 1059, Presbytrians 54, Weslyans 750, Congregationalists 2,230, other Christians 26. These figures include Punakari, Tunnukkai and Karaichchi.

Chapter IV.

TAMIL LANGUAGE AND LITERATURE.

General. Tamil is the leading language of the Dravidian family. Mr. Arunachalam writes*—"As in the case of Sanskrit, it is not possible to say when Tamil became a literary language. But while Sanskrit is a dead language and spoken only by scholars, Tamil which is so old that its words have passed into the Old Testament of the Hebrews, continnes to be the vigorous living speech of eighteen millions of people. From a very early period they have cultivated their language with such earnestness and assiduity that (in the opinion of Bishop Caldwell, the Grammarian of the Dravidian languages) 'it is impossible for any European who has acquired a competent knowledge of Tamil to regard otherwise than with respect the intellectual capacity of a people amongst whom so wonderful an organ of thought has been developed.' Its literature is in its best periods characterised by 'enthusiasm for Tamilic purity and literary independence' and 'is the only vernacular literature in India which has not been content with imitating Sanscrit, but has honourably attempted to emulate and outshine it.'"

"The language and literature were under the Pandyan kings the special charge of an academy of poets and Savants analogous to the *Academie Francaise*, and the three epochs of the academy are the great land marks in ancient Tamil history. The literature of the

* See Report on the Census of 1901. vol. i. p. 80.

first two epochs has perished, save one work, a grammar called *Tolkappiam*, and which is to Tamil what *Paniniyam* (*ashtadhyayi*) is to Sanscrit. The loss of the literature is attributed to the destruction, by the sea, at successive periods, of the two earliest Pandyan capitals old Madura and Kapadapuram. Of the works of the third epoch, which have survived, the best known is the *Kural* of *Tiruvalluvar*, a poem of singular literary and ethical value, which has been translated into most European languages."

. . . .

"The chief contribution of the Tamils to philosophy and religion is the *Saiva Siddhanta* system, which the learned Dr. Pope regards as the most influential and undoubtedly the most intrinsically valuable of the religions of India." This attempt to solve the problems of God, the soul, humanity, nature, evil, suffering, and the unseen world, has never been fully expanded in a European language, except in some measure by Dr. Pope himself, and is little known to Western scholars and divines. There is an extensive literature of esoteric philosophy attributed to an ancient brotherhood of adepts of whom the Saint Agastya is the reputed chief, and whose seat is the mountain range of Agastya Kutam in Tinnevelli district (in India.) 'So great and extensive has been their influence that the Tamil literature is permeated with esoteric truths in all its ramifications, and a vast mass of proverbs and popular songs circulating among the Tamils to-day conceals under frivolous guise profound truth'. The grammar too, is linked to the occult philosophy of the people. A large number of works on astrology, magic, and other black arts exist, which have a great vogue among certain classes of the population. These works have extended their baneful influence to Ceylon, and are among the chief authorities for the practices of demonism among the Singhalese."

It will be out of place here to allude to the long succession of brilliant Tamil poets and philosophers of South India. We shall content ourselves with referring shortly to the Jaffna poets and scholars. No mention however is made of living authors and scholars of whom there are many.

Jaffna poets. The first Jaffna poet was, of course the famous *Yalpady*, but unfortunately no specimen of his muse has been handed down to posterity. The second Jaffna poet of importance was Puvanagavago, prime minister of the first king and founder of the Nallore KandaSwamy temple, whose impromptu stanza sung at the dinner given to himself and to the king at Maviddapuram by Chinnamanatular is well known to the Jaffna Tamil scholar.

Thus the history of Jaffna began very auspiciously, as far as poets and poetry were concerned; but although there is a history of 19 centuries to record and although an unbroken line of Tamil kings exercised their benign influence over Tamil literature till the time of the Portuguese conquest, yet out of about 75 poets of Jaffna whose names are recorded in the *Galaxy of Tamil Poets* by the late Mr. Arnold, not even half a dozen can be assigned to the period intervening between the time of the first king and that of the last two centuries, so that we must conclude either that there was a sad deficiency in the number of poets worthy of the name in the land for sixteen centuries together, or that time has swept away all reminiscences of the Tamil literature of this long period

The names of Pararasasekaram and Arasakesari are the bright lights shining during this long dark interval. These poets were both of royal blood, and lived towards the close of the Tamil dynasty. The former was the first son of King Kanagasooriasinghaiaryan and is well known as the author of a poetical treatise on medicine, called Pararagasekaram,* consisting of 1,500 stanzas. The latter was the son-in-law of King Pararasasekaram and his epic poem called *Raguvamsam* narrates the history of king Ragu of Oude, an ancestor of the hero of *Ramayana.* It contains 2,404 stanzas and is highly prized.

Among modern poets we find a lawyer by the name of Senathyrayamuthaly who practised in the courts of Jaffna in the early part of last century and who composed two poems called *Nallaivenba* and *Nallaikkuravanchy* a Roman Catholic called Don Philip who was the author of *GnananathaPuranam*, an epitome of Bible history consisting of 1,104 stanzas and Mailvaganam of Pandeteruppu author of *Yalpanavaipavamalai* of *Puliyuranthathy*, who died about 175 years ago.

Among the local dramas of note are the following:

Alleynadakam by Ramasamyayer of Vaddukkoddai.

Thamaianthivilasam by Ramalingam of Anaicottai.

Alangararupanadakam and *Valapimanadakam* by Kanapatiar of Vaddukkoddai.

Kandynadakam by Kanapadipillai of Nellore, father of the late Arumuga Navelar.

Patheviravilasam by Barr Kumarakulasingha-Mudaliar of Tellipalai.

Pulantharanadakam by Coomarasamypulavar of Udupitty.

Indirakumaranapakam by Coomarasamy Mudaliar father the late Mr. C. W. Katiravelpillai of the C. C. S.

---

* An ola book consisting of many thousands of stanzas is in possession of a gentleman at Averangal who does not wish to publish it nor would he like any others to do so.

Ramanadakam and *Dharmaputranadakam* by Swaminather of Manippay.

Esthervilasam by Henry Martin of Pettah, Jaffna.

Besides the above and numerous other dramas, Jaffna has produced several *Puranams* or historical poems, such as *Soothupuranam* by Appukuddyayer of Nallore, *Koddupuranam* (on the evils of litigation) by Ramalingam of Kopay, and *Tiruvakupuranam* (Bible history) by Evarts Kanagasabaipillai of Alaveddy.

Among those who lately died must be mentioned the names of William Nevins, *alias*, Sithamparappillai, author of a poetical treatise on logic, Stansbury Kasinathar, author of an epitome of the *Ramayana*, and J. R. Arnold *alias* Sathasivampillai author of several poems such as *Meyvethasaram* (essence of true Vedam), *Nanerikkothu* (a moral poem), Tiruchatakam (on Christ), *Gnanavenba* (on wisdom) and of numerous Christian lyrics.

Prose Writers. Among prose works published by Jaffna scholars, those by Arumuga Navalar form a large proportion. His *Periapuranavasanam*, (history of the 63 Hindu Saints) his "*Palapadam*," (reading books for children,) "*Ilakkanackchurukkam*" (a work on Tamil grammar) and a host of others readily occur to the mind of the average student. Mr. Santhirasekara Pandither of Uduvil has with the help derived from the manuscripts of a Tamil—English Dictionary prepared by Mr. Knight of the Church Mission, laid the Tamil speaking population under obligation by producing a useful dictionary. Mr. C. W. Katiravelpillai's great work in the same direction has recently appeared in the form of an accurate and elaborate Tamil Dictionary on a European basis. His treatise on logic also deserves mention. Mr. S. S. Jeremiah of Araly has produced a series of Tamil readers, well worthy of the name. Rev. S. John has produced a history of Jaffna. Mr. J. R. Arnold's chief works in prose are his *Galaxy of Tamil Poets*, *Moral Tales* and a *Universal Compend of Astronomy*.

Among the foreigners who with the assistance of Tamil scholars in Jaffna have enriched our literature must be mentioned Dr. M. Winslow whose Tamil-English dictionary is an admitted authority, and Dr. S. F. Green who published various medical works in Tamil, mainly translations from English.

It is indeed a regrettable fact that that many a worthy Tamil work has not seen the light through the press, and that many have probably been lost altogether. True it is we have had no Shakesphere or Milton, true it is that Kampar Kachchiappar were of India, but admittedly we have had poets of eminence and sufficient celebrity. A plea for the revival of Tamil literature cannot therefore he out of place in these pages.

Chapter V.

EDUCATION.

The official returns shew that the percentage of the school going population in the Peninsula compares favourably with that of many a cultured European country. There is a desire for learning inherent in the Tamil race which not even the most abject poverty can extinguish. The country is liberally supplied with schools and colleges.

Mr. Ievers writes: "Education is spreading. No other district possesses such a large number of educational institutions as Jaffna, which has six Colleges, as a natural consequence of the invasion of Western ideas of thought and feeling, real or supposed to be real. The primitive habits and customs of the people are fast dying out, a result which, in my opinion, is far from satisfactory.

The Jaffna College, situated at Vaddukkoddai 7 miles from Jaffna Town, stands foremost as a first grade college.* It is the revival of the far famed Batticotta Seminary which was started in 1823. About 15 years after the Seminary was closed by the American Board the more prominent of its old boys desiring its resuscitation collected funds and started the Jaffna College on the 3rd July, 1872 with the substantial support of the American Mission.

---

*Trinity College in Kandy is also a first grade College but has not as yet sent a single student for the B. A. degree.

It is incorporated by Ordinance No. 7 of 1894 and is controlled by a Board of Directors. It is independent of Government support and has a splendid gymnasium and laboratory which are second to none in the Island. It has over forty free scholarships and is the only college which in imitation of the Universities of the West insists on her students residing in the premises. It has no school department but admits students from the pre-matriculation class to the B. A. Standard.

Jaffna Hindu College is a national undertaking started independently of any missionary or European support. It is within 1½ miles from the town and sends in students for the First in Arts Examination. It is incorporated by ordinance No. 6 of 1902 and is controlled by a Board of Directors.

It had its beginning in a school formed by the late Mr. Wm. Nevins *alias* Sidamparappillai on his severing his connection with the Wesleyan Central College of which he had been the headmaster. This school was developed into a College in September 1895, mainly through the exertions of the late Mr. Adv. Nagalingam who raised funds for the erection of a suitable building. The College is provided with an efficient staff of teachers with Mr. Nevins Selvaduraipillai B.A. as Principal.

St. Patrick's College is an institution which is not in favour of the Indian University examinations, and confines its operations to preparing students for the Cambridge locals. It is within 1½ miles of the fort and is under the Roman Catholic Bishop of Jaffna.

Jaffna Central College is situated at Vempady close to the Esplanade and is under the Wesleyan management. It prepares students for the First in Arts examination. Its chief feeders are the Pt. Pedro High School and the Chetty Street School.

St. John's College is situated at Chundiculy close to the

Jaffna Kachcheri. It is under the Church Missionary Society and prepares students for the Cambridge locals as well as for the Calcutta examinations.

Victoria College is due entirely to private enterprise, Mr. C. M. Chellappah and his brother Mr. C. M Duraiappah being the promoters and proprietors This College was started in commemoration of the diamond jubilee of our late Queen Victoria. It is situated at Chulipuram about 9 miles from Jaffna.

BOARDING SCHOOLS FOR GIRLS.

The Girls' Boarding School at Uduvil, under the Management of the American Mission, is the oldest institution of its kind in Jaffna and perhaps in Ceylon having been started in 1826. English and Tamil are taught there. Candidates are sent in for the Calcutta and Cambridge examinations. The *Udapitty Girls' Boarding School* has lately been amalgamated with the Uduvil institution.

Vempadi Girls' Boarding School is managed by the Weslyan Mission and instruction is imparted in English and Tamil on the same lines as at Uduvil.

Chundiculy Girls' High School under the C. M. Society sends pupils for the Cambridge local and the Calcutta Entrance. It is also a boarding school.

Nallore Grils' Boarding School is under the same Society and most of the classes are in Tamil.

CONVENTS.

There is one asylum under the Roman Catholic Mission for housing poor orphan girls. The girls orphanage at Main Street Jaffna in managed by European Nuns and there is also attached to the Institution a Native Society of Nuns which supplies the Girls' Schools under the Mission with the necessary staff of teachers. A flourishing branch of this society has been established at Ilavalai. This is supported by a European Society called the "Holy Childhood."

INDUSTRIAL SCHOOLS.

The Tellipalai Industrial School under the American Mission trains over 100 boys in printing, bookbinding and carpentry. There is in connection with this school the largest and best equipped press in Jaffna. It was here that this hand-book was printed.

Colombogam Industrial School attached to the Colombogam orphanage is a training school for teachers and an Industrial school where carpentry and printing are taught. It is under the R. C. Mission.

Besides the above Institutions there are a number of English and Vernacular high and middle schools most of them brought under the Government grant-in-aid system. Almost every village can boast of at least one vernacular school.

Chapter VI.

JOURNALISM.

It is worthy of remark that Jaffna, though condemned by many as benighted, ranks second only to Colombo in point of journalism.

NEWSPAPERS.

The Morning Star, English and Tamil, started in 1840 is now under the editorial control of a representative committee from the American, Church and Wesleyan Missions. The proprietor is Mr. T. S. Cooke, Proctor, Jaffna. It was once a fortnightly, but is now a weekly, printed at Tellipalai.

The Ceylon Patriot started in 1863 by Mr. C. W. Katiravelpillai, then practising as an Advocate, is a weekly and is edited by Mr. H. F. Johnpulle who is also the manager and proprietor.

The Jaffna Catholic Guardian started in 1876 by Dr. Bonjean as the organ of the Roman Catholic body is now printed in English and Tamil as two separate papers. The English weekly is edited by Mr. J. H. Martyn and the Tamil fortnightly by Mr. F. Tamboo. Rev. Groussault is the manager and proprietor.

Sanmarkapothini is a Tamil monthly edited by Mr S. Tambimuttu. It was started in 1884 and is printed at Achchuvely.

The Hindu Organ started in 1889 as an English and Tamil fortnightly is now published separately. The English weekly is edited by Mr. A. Sabapathy, the Tamil fortnightly by Mr. P. Kartigasu. The "Saiva Paripalana Sabai" is the manager and proprietor.

Suthasanadium is a Tamil fortnightly started in 1901 and is edited by Mr. K. Velupillai who is also the proprietor and manager. It is printed at Vasavilan.

MAGAZINES.

The Jaffna College Miscellany appears three times a year and was started in 1872.

Victoria College Magazine is a quarterly started in 1898.

The Central is a quarterly Magazine of the Jaffna Central College. It was started in 1900.

The Ceylon Law Review is a monthly started in 1901. It is edited by Mr. Isaac Tambyah, Advocate.

The Christian Review is a quarterly started in 1904. It is edited by Mr. Isaac Tambyah, Advocate.

St. John's College Magazine was started in 1904 under the auspices of the Old Boys Association of the College. It is a quarterly.

Chapter VII.

AGRICULTURE.

Says Sir Emerson Tennent, "the perfection of the village cultivation is truly remarkable, it is horticulture rather than agriculture, and reminds one of the market gardens of Falham and Chelsea more forcibly than anything I have seen out of England."

The soil is responsive to systematic cultivation and is but imperfectly adapted for maintaining a constant succession of seeds and cereal production.

Wells. The value of wells is extreme in a country like this, where rivers and even the smallest streams are unknown, and where the cultivators are entirely dependent on the rains of the two monsoons. From the wells labourers raise water by means of buckets (mostly woven of palmyrah leaves and called *Paddai*) attached to horizontal levers called *Thulah* by a long rope. Two persons at least and very often more are required at each well; one or more of them walk forward and back along the *thulah* which would be about as long as the depth of the well, whilst the other one below directs the *paddai* in its descent into the well and again in its ascent, and empties it at the head of the conducting channel.

The wells are numerous and almost every garden and dwelling compound has one or more each. We find fresh water wells even by the sea-side. The coral *stratum* in which the well is sunk is porous. It has been discovered "that water containing considerable quantities of saline matter in solution may, by merely percolating through great masses of porous *strata* during long periods, be gradually deprived of its salt to such an extent as to render even sea water fresh." This discovery proves true in the case of most of our wells. It is very often the case that the wells are below sea level and most of them are not effected by any drought. The water in and about the Town of Jaffna is brackish.

The Puttur tidal well and **Uralu** well called **Pokkanai** are regarded as natural curiosities in that they differ from ordinary wells both as regards the volume of water they contain and other peculiarities. Sir E. Tennent writes :—"Near Puttur, at a place called Navakeeri, there is a remarkable well, which is one of the wonders of the Peninsula. It occurs in a bed of stratified limestone, so hollow that in passing over it the footsteps of our horses sounded as though they were striking on an arch. The well is about 30ft in diameter, and sinks to a depth of four-and-twenty fathoms On the surface it is fresh, but lower down it is brackish and salt, and on plunging a bottle to the extreme depth, the water came up highly fœtid, and giving off bubbles of sulphuretted hydrogen gas. But the most remarkable fact connected with this well is that its surface rises and falls a few inches once in every twenty four hours, but it never overflows its banks and is never reduced below a certain fixed point, even by the abstraction of large quantities of water." On two occasions, once in 1824 and again in 1897, steam engines erected at the well failed to lower the water level in any perceptible degree. The first experiment was made with an intention of irrigating the surrounding districts, the second with the intention of supplying water to the town. The experiments failed, the one owing to the rocky state of the surrounding lands and the other owing to the bad water.

The well at Uralu has its own history. In sinking it the workmen came upon the limestone rock which gave way and shewed a cavern below containing the water they were in search of, with a depth of 33 feet. The wells are uninfluenced by rains or droughts.

The Sinking of the Earth at Manippay. On Friday the 19th May 1905, at Navaly near Manippay, a small opening was found and it continued to enlarge covering an area of over one fourth of a rood. The water is about 40ft deep and is salt. It is within one or two feet of the ground level. It is presumed that this new circular pit has the same connection with the sea as the old rectangular pit at Puttur.

Rice. In spite of all the difficulties of soil and irrigation a large quantity of rice is grown though not enough for the actual consumption of the inhabitants. The Tamil invaders are said to have disturbed the control of the tanks in the Wanny and consequently the people had to depend on India for their supply of paddy and rice—a dependence which has contin ed unrelieved up to the present day. The agricultural company started in 1902 with a view to buy Crown lands at Paranthan and to cultivate rice there was liquidated in May 1905 owing to the severe conditions imposed on it by Government.

Dry grains. There are 12 different kinds of dry grains the chief of which are *varago, kurakkan, millet, mondy, chamy, gram, pulse, peas, and gingilee.* They are grown in the fields, some of them during the season of rice cultivation and others at other seasons also. The season for rice cultivation is from August to February.

Vegetables. Onions, chillies, turmeric, ginger, pumpkins, brinjals, gourds, spinac, melons, yams, sweet-potatoes, keerai (pot herb or country cabbage) arrowroot, tapioca are grown and are specially well cultivated in gardens.

Potatoes, cabbages, carrots, turnips, and lettuce are successfully grown though the yield is not very encouraging. Tomatoes thrive very well.

There is a kind of yam called the *King-yam* (*Irasavallikkilango* in Tamil) peculiar to Valigamam North. The yam when boiled in diluted coconut juice adding just a little sugar, gives it a delicious taste. Europeans like it immensely. The yams keep well without rotting for an year and even over.

Betel-vine, and lime, orange, plantain and arecanut trees thrive well if carefully attended to. *Papawa* and *Bilimbi* are also found in the Town.

Breadfruit tree is propagated from the roots. It grows but not freely and requires constant watering.

Jak fruits which weigh from 3 to 60 pounds are said to be the largest eatable fruits in the world: they spring from the rugged surface of the tree and are suspended by a powerful stalk which attaches itself to the trunk. The jak tree in Jaffna unlike that in the Singhalese district has to be carefully watered.

Grape vine has been successfully grown in the Jaffna Town during the last 200 years. It has been recently introduced into Mathakal, Sillalay and other villages where it is found to grow even better than in Jaffna. More extensive and systematic cultivation is to be recommended in view of its being always marketable with the railway now running to Colombo. "Some trees in Colombo treated by a Jaffna gardener have produced fair crops." The Jaffna vine was probably brought by the Dutch from Negapatam for that proved identical with the Muscat vine obtained by Mr. Dyke in 1840.

Some Australian grape seeds, which were deposited in the garden by way of experiment by the writer, began to grow. Two of those plants are still growing, but they require some shade and ample water. When exposed to the sun the tender leaves begin to wither. The growth of the vine for the last four months is only 3 feet.

The Ground-nut, the cultivation of which was specially recommended by the present Governor and about which much has been said in the papers was tried by the writer. With all deference to men of superior judgment and experience in such matters he desires to state that the result of his own experiment on a very small scale was far from satisfactory, the return being not even three-fold of the seed planted. However he would be glad to know that this poor result was due rather to the particular soil on which he tried it, which was hard and clayey than to the unsuitability of its cultivation to the Jaffna soil in general.

Pine apples grow well in the Eastern part of the Peninsula.

Pomegranates are not extensively grown, a few trees being grown here and there and in gardens attached to dwelling houses. Some of the fruit is very sour and is used for medical purposes.

Mangoes grow from seeds. Grafts are made from valuable kinds. There are some nice varieties in the Kachcheri garden. A particular kind is called here the *Colombo Mango,* whereas the identical one is called in Colombo the *Jaffna Mango.* The juice of the mango, when freshly pulled "feels as cool as iced water." The fruit must be eaten instantly; even an interval of a few minutes after it has been gathered is sufficient to destroy the charm; for, once severed from the stem, it rapidly acquires the temperature of the surrounding air.

Tobacco. What Sir E. Tennent said of tobacco some 55 years ago is true of it even to this day. He says, "The grand staple of this District, and that on which the prosperity of its agriculture is chiefly dependent, is tobacco, for the excellence of which Jaffna has long been celebrated in the South of India; and at a former period it was in equal request in Sumatra, Java and the Eastern Archipelago. It is on the breadth and success of this crop that the extent and excellence of all the others are mainly dependent; for as the ground requires to be highly prepared for tobacco, two and even three crops of a less exhausting description are afterwards taken off it in succession, without additional manuring; whilst the increasing demand for tobacco causes new land to be broken up for its growth, thus stimulating a constantly progressive improvement in the culture of all the inferior lands." Many have taken to the cultivation of it. Over 15,000 acres in Jaffna are under tobacco. The usual mode of *curing* the leaf is as follows: a circular room about 7 ft. high is built of mud and to the ceiling are closely hung the leaves cut the day previous. On the floor of the room, which is a foot or two below the ground level and which has a small entrance, is burnt such combustibles as cause the largest quantity of smoke and least of flame The pith and the leaf stalks of the palmyrah and cocoanut trees are about the best for the purpose. After exposing the leaves for about 12 hours to such smoke and fire they are gathered and heaped up. A day or two afterwards the same process is repeated and the tobacco is ready for the market. For cigars and how to make them, see next chapter.

Both as regards the growing and curing of local tobacco need is felt of scientific improvement with a view to render the leaf acceptable to the great markets of the world. If this acceptability is secured a very powerful impulse would be given to the systematic cultivation of the weed on a very large scale and tobacco will in all probability be as great a staple industry and go as much to the making of the Island as tea.

The Cocoanut* palm (*Cocos nucifera*) is extensively grown in many parts of the Peninsula. It requires special attention. In the hot season watering is essential for young plants and for older ones too in times of long drought. The timber is not half as good as that of the palmyrah, but the products, oil, punnac, coir etc. give a better return to capitalists. With exceptionally good soil and other favorable conditions a plant may come into bearing in five years, but as a general rule it takes at least ten years of watering and tending before it begins to give a return. Some varieties of Batavian and Maldivian cocoanuts are also grown.

Toddy is extensively drawn from the cocoanut palm all the year round.

Cocoanut cultivation on a systematic scale was started early in the forties of the last century by such European pioneers as Mr. Hardy, and in the course of time several estates were formed especially in the Pachchilapaly Division of the Peninsula. Many of these estates, originally under European management, have gradually passed into the hands of the Jaffnese. Most of the crown land available in the Peninsula have been purchased and cocoanut planting is pursued by the Jaffnese almost as a rage. Clearings have also been made at Veddukkadu, between, Punakari and

---

* "The name *Cocoa* seems to be a contraction of the Portuguese *Macoco* or *Macaco*, a monkey, and to have been given from the resemblance between the end of the shell, where the three black scars are, and the face of a monkey."
Penny Cyclopaedia.

Calmunai, in the mainland where a few estates have come into bearing while others are being planted.

The Palmyrah palm *(Borassus flabelliformis)* retains the name *palmeira brava* bestowed on it by the Portuguese. It grows not only in the Northern part of Ceylon but also in the Southern part of India. It is also to be met with as a natural curiosity in the Straits Settlements, in some of the Islands of the Malay Archipalago, in Arabia and even in Gibraltar where travellers say there is a solitary tree. It requires but little labour and cultivation, except that of planting the nuts and protecting them from cattle till they grow above their reach. The growth of the tree is very slow and it takes from 15 to 30 years to bear. It is a very useful palm. There are two kinds of the palmyrah *viz*, the male and the female. The male tree bears no fruit, but both are used for drawing toddy.

The palmyra toddy is sweet when quite fresh, but bitter when fermentation sets in. The toddy season is from January to August. The spathes of the palmyrah trees exhibit themselves in January and the toddy-drawer forthwith commences his operations, climbing by the assistance of a loop of *naar* of the palmyrah stalk, sufficiently wide to admit both his ankles and leave a space between them, thus enabling him to grasp the trunk of the tree with his feet, and support himself as he ascends. Having cleansed the crown from old leaves and fruit stalks and other superfluous matter, he binds the spathes tightly with thongs to prevent them from further expansion, and descends, after having thoroughly bruised the embrayo flowers within to facilitate the exit of juice. For several mornings the operation of crushing is repeated, and each time a slice is taken off the end of the racemes to facilitate the exit of the sap, and prevent its bursting the spathe. In about a week the sap begins to exude. On ascertaining that the first flow of the sap has taken place, the toddy drawer again trims the wounded spathe, and inserts its extremity in an earthen pot, called *muddy*, to collect the juice. The *muddy* is tied up to the spathe. Morning and evening these vessels are emptied, and for a period of six months the palmyrah will continue to pour forth its sap at the rate of two to four quarts a day· The juice if permitted to ferment, is a slightly intoxicating and unpalatable drink. What cheap drinks such as beer and porter are to the people of Europe toddy is to the people of Ceylon. Toddy in Tamil is called *Kallu*.

To sweeten the toddy a little lime is put into the pot before it is tied up to the spathe. The sweetened toddy is called *Karuppany.* If intended to be made into *jaggery (Panamkaddy)*, the sweetened toddy, after being boiled down to the consistency of syrup is poured into small baskets made of palmyrah leaf (called *Kuddan*), where it cools, and a partial crystalisation ensues. If the syrup is of a lighter consistency than jaggery it is called *pany* which retains its fluid state for years even if cooled. In it is preserved the palmyrah jelly.

If the vessel for drawing toddy which is usually earthen is well cleaned and dried in the sun or heated in the fire before it is attached to the spathe the juice flowing into it is called *Neera* a very delicious and refreshing drink. *Karuppany* owing to the existence of lime is not so cooling as *Neera*, nevertheless it is agreeable to the taste.

The juice of the palmyrah fruit though not very palatable at first to the foreigner has been extensively used by the poor classes as food. It is also spread on mats and dried in the sun and cut up into slices in which form it is preserved for months and used with other food. This jelly is called *Panattu* in Tamil. Mixed with the *pany* these slices will last for years and the writer has known some foreigners who have taken a great liking to them. The palmyrah fruit however is not very nutritious and even among the poor it is not used extensively as food as in former days.

The seeds, if planted, germinate in three months or so and in the first stages of growth it forms into a pulpy substance called *Kilangoe* which is also used as food.

The wood of a fairly old tree is hard, strong and durable and is generally used for roofing. The leaf when green is a good food for black cattle. The leaf is largely used for covering the roof and for screening the fence. Ola books, fans, umbrellas and baskets are made of it. The fibre is used for making brushes. The ridge of the leaf called *Ekku* and the polished cover of the stalk called *Naar* are used for making ropes.

The Tamarind tree,*(tamarindus Indica)*is one of spontaneous growth. It is grown for the sake of its shade and for its fruit. The trunk of the tree is lofty, large, and crowned with wide spreading branches; the flowers are in simple clusters, terminating the short lateral branches. The fruit is very much used for preparing native curry. It abounds with an acid pulp possessed of refrigerant and laxative properties. The trunk of the tree is used for making the native oil mill described in the next Chapter.

The Margosa tree *(Melia)* is a Portuguese name for *Vempu* in Tamil. It grows to a good height and the timber is highly valued. Its bark is bitter and used as a tonic. A valuable oil is expressed from its seeds, and a tenacious gum exudes from its trunk. The oil is undoubtedly efficacious and almost antiseptic. The bark, the leaves and the oil have the properties of counter-acting the effects of malaria. The wood is white-ant proof.

The tree grows spontaneously and in view of its durable timber, its excellent shade and its anti-malarial effects, the Railway and P. W. D. authorities will do well to plant them on either side of the long line and road through the malarial region of the Wanny. At the Railway stations and the Rest Houses too, a number of trees may be planted with advantage for the same reason.

The Suria tree (*Thespesia populnea*) also known as the "Tulip" or "Portia" tree, supplies the wood commonly in demand for cart wheel. Tho wood is not obtainable in large quantities. The tree is generally used here for live-fence as is *Kiluvay*.

The Iluppai tree (*Bassia longifolia*) is found largely at Averangal. The oil is good for rheumatic patients. The wood resembles iron-wood and stands any amount of use under water. The oil is used at times to adulterate ghee.

Chapter VIII.

INDUSTRIES AND OCCUPATIONS.

Machinery for any industry is practically unknown in this part of the Island. All the manufactures turned out by the people are the results of handi craft. It is strange that even after a century of British rule, the people have not been initiated into the mysteries of machinery. Telling them that they must make a start themselves is like asking them to make bricks without straw, for it is a well known fact that the wealth of the country is very limited. Even in a prosperous country like Japan the Government had to introduce machinery into all the departments of manual labour and work them at their own expense till the efforts of private speculators relieved them of this duty. If the Government of Japan had followed our local Government its position at present would have been different.

We have dealt with agriculture, the chief industry, in Chapter vii.

DYEING.

The process of dyeing in this country is as laborious as it is unique. The impliments used are but few; nevertheless the work is so admirable that it has taxed the ingenuity of many who are curious to know.

The cloth to be dyed is first washed well and then dipped in water mixed with the flour derived from the palmyrah root (called *Odeal* or dried *Kilangoe*.) With an instrument called *Kammiathuriakal**, bee-wax is applied on both sides of the lines that are to be formed on the borders of the cloth.

Achchukaddyneelam, i. e. blue pressed into cakes and sold at Rs, 3 a pound, is dissolved in water by being kept for two or three days running. *Thakaraikoddai* (*Kassia Tora* seed) is boiled in water. *Thillai* (*Excœcaria agalloka*) is burnt to ashes and water mixed with it is allowed to filter into a vessel. All the above three preparations are mixed in equal proportions and applied on the space between the two lines of bee-wax, thus a new blue line is formed in the centre. The cloth is allowed to dry and the mixture is reapplied and dried.

Now the wax is taken out by putting the cloth in boiling water. Then the borders of the cloth are dipped in water mixed with Indian gall-nut reduced to powder. The cloth is again dried and the sides of the lines already formed are rewaxed. Alum mixed with water is then applied to the lines. In some cases iron rust is mixed with the alum to make the line darker. The use of iron is bad as it corrodes the cloth. The cloth is now dipped two or three times into water in which the dyer's root called *chaya* root is kept boiling. After this process the cloth is washed in water (salt water preferred) and allowed to dry in the shade. The cloth generally called *neelakampiveddy* thus becomes ready for the market.

The ordinary dyed cloth is done without the elaborate process that is required to produce the blue lines.

Any ornamental work on the lines is done by the wax being so applied as to leave space of the required figure or impression. The different tints are produced by

* This instrument looks like a trident, the three ends of which are joined by a bar. Thread is run round it to make it retain wax. Literally it means the brush of a painter.

powders of different colours being mixed with the *chaya* root.

A spurious syrup or powder which when first applied gives a freshness and beauty to the cloth but which fades away and disappears after the 2nd or 3rd wash is now generally used as a substitute for the *chaya* root.

The average Jaffna man generally uses this dyed cloth and the reason is that it wears better and lasts longer than the white cloth.

The cost for dyeing a cloth 4 yards long varies from 40 cents to Rs. 10. The cost increases according to the neatness, nicety and the elaborate character of the work turned out.

OIL MILLS.

European machinery worked by steam power for expressing oil is unknown in this part of the Island. The mills, however, locally designed fairly meet the requirements.

The crushing of copra* and the *gingilee*, *Iluppai* and other seeds for the expression of the oil is one of the industries of the place. A *chekku* or a creaking mill, so called from the disagreeable noise it produces, is erected for this purpose. It consists of a large granite stone or the trunk of a tamarind tree hallowed like a mortar, in which a heavy upright pestle is worked round by bullocks yoked to a transverse beam, which rests on and moves round the stone or trunk which is buried deep and firm as to be able to stand the resulting pressure.

In some cases a mill called *Uttumaram* is formed out of two beams which are fitted loose into two up-

* Copra is dried cocoanut. It is prepared by taking the husk off the fruit and then breaking open the nut and exposing the kernel to the sun. In 3 or 4 days the kernel easily separates from the shell. It is allowed to dry a day or more longer when it would be ready for the mill.

right posts. Between the two beams is put the seed within an ola basket called *Uttuppeddy.* The two beams are now pressed hard against each other with the help of a lever attached to a rope passing round the two beams one end being fixed to one of the posts.

WEAVING

is conducted by two classes of people, the Kaikolas and the Cheniars. Now some of the Pariahs also have learnt to weave certain kinds of cloths bearing their name.

The Jaffna weaver takes his station under a shed where he stretches his warp thread (called *Nesavupa*) between two wooden rollers which are fastened to the floor by wooden pins. He digs a hole in the earth large enough to contain his legs when in a sitting posture; and then suspending to a rafter of the roof the cords which are intended to cause the raising and depressing of the warp threads, he fixes underneath two loops for his toes by which he produces a substitute for treadles. His shuttle acts also as a batten or lay and completes his simple arrangements.

The first operation called warping consists in laying the requisite number of threads together to form the width of the cloth. In the language of the weavers the warp threads are the long threads and the weft (called *Udu*) are the cross threads. The yarn wound in the bobbins as it leaves the hand of the spinner is stretched at full length in an open field. Supposing there are to be five hundred threads in the width of a piece of cloth, the threads unwound and laid out are arranged into five hundred parallel lengths constituting the warp of the intended cloth.

The shuttle with the weft thread passing through the alternate raisings and depressings of the threads forward and backward is worked by the weaver who at the same time works the batten and the loops that lift and depress the threads alternately.

It is a matter for regret that these industrious people should continue to be satisfied with the rude apparatus that has been handed down to them by their ancestors.

CIGAR MAKING.

This is one of the paying industries of Jaffna. The Jaffna cigar has already gained a name for itself, and has been the recepient of a gold medal at the St. Louis Exhibition, 1904.

Cigar rolling is all done by hand. The leaf is torn into pieces. Bits of the inferior variety of tobacco are rolled between the hands and then enveloped with a piece of the superior variety called the covering leaf and fastened by a thread. There is a stick cut to measurement. The roll is put by its side and the outflanking leaves are cut off by a pair of scissors. These cigars are made into bundles of ten each. The bundles are pressed hard into a box. A decoction called *Koda** is sprinkled over each layer which gives both strength and flavour to the cigars impregnated with it in the course of a few weeks.

At a meeting held at the Colombo Library in 1889 in favour of the Railway Extension to the North, Mr. Advocate Dornhorst K. C., was reported to have incidentally remarked that Jaffna cigars had attractive peculiarities of their own. The only objection to them being that they should be smoked in private, when they are even more enjoyable—a remark which was fully endorsed by another speaker the Hon. Mr. S. C. Obeyasekare.

---

*Koda is prepared by the ribs of the tobacco leaf being boiled continually for two or three days. To this then is added arrack, sugar and spices.

The cost of making 1000 cigars is from 60 cents to a rupee. An expert and a small boy could finish the 1000 in 8 hours.

The growing and the curing of the leaf has been noticed in the previous chapter.

BASKET AND MAT MAKING.

Baskets are made of palmyrah leaves and are of various kinds and dimensions. The required olas are prepared out of tender leaves which are dried in the shade. This manufacture is largely done in Wadamerachy and in the Islands.

The person who works at the baskets brings together all the olas and squats on the floor. The rib of the leaf is torn out with a style which is practically the handle of a knife with a curved blade, called *Kampoochuttukam*—the only tool used. As the rib is separated, a small folded bit, technically called *Kaddithal* clasps the breadth of the long leaf and the blade applied to a cut in the *Kaddithal* severs the long leaf according to the breadth required. This process is called *Varuthal.* A certain number of these prepared leaves called *ethals* are laid out lengthwise and are temporarily tied together with some fibres to keep them in position.

The process of interweaving these leaves is very much like the working of the warp thread and the weft thread in weaving. For at alternate liftings of leaves spread out lengthwise, the cross ones are laid.

The corners are formed by turning the "wrap" leaves into "weft" leaves. A specially made basket called *paddai* serves as bucket for drawing water. It is made water-tight by doubling the *ethals* and closing them in as often and as well as possible. As the leaves have a tendency to expand when brought into contact with water the bucket becomes all the more water-tight.

Sometimes the baskets and the mats are interlaced with dyed leaves called *Chaya ola.* They help to make some lovely ornamental works highly prized by foreigners.

A good deal of fancy work is done with the help of these olas. It mostly occupies the time of females who work at it with a deal of pleasure just as sewing and stitching occupies the European women.

GOLDSMITHS.

Sir Emerson Tennent says, "The goldsmiths (of Jaffna) are ingenious and excellent workmen and produce bangles, chains and rings whose execution is as fine as their designs are tasteful. Nothing is more interesting than to watch one of these primitive artists at his occupation seated in the open air, with no other apparatus than a few clumpsy tools, a blow pipe, and a *chatty* full of sand on which to light his charcoal fire."

Many distinguished Europeans have taken away with them fine specimens of the work of the Jaffna handicraftsman and among these the most distinguished is H. M. King Edward VII who on his visit to Ceylon in 1875 as H. R. H. the Prince of Wales graciously accepted some of the finest jewelry enclosed in a silver casket made by Jaffna goldsmiths under the special direction of Sir Wm. Twynam, then Government Agent.

OCCUPATIONS.

The following list shows how most of the Jaffna bread winners are occupied. The numbers marked against the different headings shew the number of persons engaged as the names indicate. For the convenience of the reader they are alphabetically arranged.

Occupation	Number
Actors, Singers etc.,	137
Agriculturists either as landowners or cultivators	49,606
Barbers	695
Beggers	141
Blacksmiths	1909
Boatmen	456
Butchers	15
Carpenters	1,475
Cart-drivers	499
Cigar makers	1893
Cowherds & Shepherds	790
Dhobies	1747
Doctors & Apothecaries	54
Drapers	250
Dyers	201
Farriers	2
Fishermen	6,267
Flower garland makers and Sellers	124
Goldsmiths	3036
Government employees	760
Labourers	1633
Lawyers	53
Lawyer's Clerks	57
Masons	348
Merchants	708
Missionaries & Clergymen	42
Notaries	35
Pensioners	285
Potters	172
Priests (Hindu)	516
Tavernkeepers (Toddy and arrack)	63
Teachers	598
Toddy drawers	3545
Weavers	678

Wiythiar (men practicing medicine without going much into the science of it, but working on established formulae) 333.

Chapter IX.

THINGS OF INTEREST.

RUINS.

We find scattered all over the Peninsula, ruins of several buildings and some of which are of great interest

The ruined Portuguese fort at **Kaits** called *Fort Eyrie* lies on the shore opposite Fort Hammanhiel. which rises at the entrance of the Kaits port.

At **Velanai** may be seen a heap of stones probably the remains of an old Portuguese or Dutch tower. The tower was in existence in 1832 and was 50 feet high.

At a place called *Sangily toppu* at **Nallore** beyond the 2nd mile post on the Jaffna—Pt. Pedro road, is found a gateway still intact which is all that remains of a palace etc., built by the first king of Jaffna.

There are seen ruins of Portuguese churches at **Atchuvely** and **Changanai**. All that is left of the ruins at Changanai is the chancel vaulted in coral stone: it is in a state of fair preservation.

At **Kangesanturai** near the Customs is an extensive foundation, probably of a Dutch fort.

At **Elephant Pass** stands the rest house on the ruins of an old Dutch fort.

Two fortresses at short distances from the Elephant Pass rest house across the isthmus were erected by the Dutch at **Pass Beschuter** and **Pass Pyl,** over the ruins of the former is a P.W.D. bungalow and rest house

CURIOSITIES.

The tidal well. at **Puttur**, the well called *Pokkanai* at **Uralu**, and the recently formed salt-water pool at Navaly near **Manipay** have been described in chapter vii, and are of great interest to scientists.

By the seaside at **Keerimalai**, two miles from Kangasanturai, freshwater springs are abundant. The sea at flood covers them and at ebb they are so exposed as to afford every facility for people to bathe and wash. The same phenomenon is noticed at **Nediakadu** within about half a mile from Valvettiturai, but it is not convenient for people to bathe or wash.

Near **Urikkadu**, a sanitary station of the American Mission, and within about three miles of Valvettiturai there is a long underground cavern called *Mandapam.*

Mr. J. P. Lewis, Govt. Agent, says that some Singhalese gold coins were found at **Vallipuram** near Point Pedro.

He also speaks of some copper coins in an earthen pot being dug up at **Pandateruppu** in Valigamam West. The spot where these were found is, according to tradition, the site of the palace of a queen. It is called *Irasamurunkaiady.* This *Murunkai (Adria cordifolia)* is said to be the only one of the kind in the Peninsula.

On a cocoanut estate planted by the late Mr. C. W. Katiravelpillai at **Punnalai** there is a curious cocoanut tree. The tree began to grow and in a short time a score of young plants sprang from the stem of the tree underground as in the case of a plantain, cane etc. Even now fresh shoots are coming up. Some of the older ones withered and died away after a few years, while others are growing and a few of these are now in bearing. This cocoanut plant is one of unique growth in the Island• there being no other instance known except perhaps one at Negombo.

Cocoanut and palmyrah trees however, with two and three branches may be met with in the Peninsula.

BULDINGS ETC., OF INTEREST.

The Jaffna Fort which was built by the Portuguese in 1632 and reconstructed by the Dutch (says Sir E. Tennent), "is the most perfect little military work in Ceylon—a pentagon built of blocks of white coral and surrounded by a moat." Within it are the king's house, some of the officers' quarters, a church* and the prison house. "It is a pentagon with ravelins; each bastion mounts 12 guns, each revel'n 6 guns; wet ditch round, four fronts scarp and counterscarp of coral masonry."

Fort Hammaphiel is a small fort erected on a rock in the harbour of Kaits a few hundred yards from the shore. It is built of coral stone and is provided with a receptacle for rain water, the bottom of which is 15 feet above sea level and which rises to a height of about 30 feet with a top of about 20 ft. square. Formerly occupied as a state prison it is now used as a quarantine station.

The Clock tower on the Esplanade to the North East of the Fort may be taken as the loyal part which the Jaffna people took in the commemoration of the visit to the Island in 1875 of the then Prince of Wales, now H. M. King Edward VII. It was with the balance of the Jaffna Prince of Wales reception fund

*The church, which is in the form of a Greek cross was by the capitulation reserved for the Presbyterian consistory, but by their courtesy it is used for the service of the Church of England. Mr. J. P. Lewis, present Govt. Agent, says that the bell was examined and was found to bear the following inscription: "N. S. Dos Milagres de Jaffna Patao." which means "Our Lady of Miracles of Jaffna patam."

that the Tower was built and the clock provided is the gift of the late Sir James Longden. The bell of the clock bears the date 1882.

Katiresankovil at Vannarponne a little beyond the grand bazaar was built by the chetties about 40 years ago. The carved work in the temple is of some interest to sight seers

A Hindu Temple. As non-Hindus are not allowed to enter a Hindu temple it may be of some interest to note the structure of Hindu temples which is all on a settled plan with slight variation in matters of details. The ground plan of a temple is given on page 55.

The *idol* or *image* is placed at the *Ketpakirakam*—the Holy of Holies. The priests perform their *pooja* from the threshold of the *Aruthamandapam.* The spices, sandal, cakes etc. necessary for the *pooja* are arranged and kept in readiness at the *Mahamandapam.* Devotees do their *Nadanam* (devotional dance) in the *Nirutthamandapam.* In the *Sthampamandapam* stand the three altars and the flagstaff called *Kodystham-pam.* Worshippers flock to this. They may go into the *Niruttamandapam* and the *Mahamandapam* but are denied all access to the *Aruthamandapam* and the *Ketpakirakam.*

The space around the temple is called *Ulveethy* or the inner court-yard. A parapet wall called *chuttu-mathil* runs round the *Ulveethy.* The main gate or entrance into the temple is generally from the East or North. The belfry is on the side of the gate which is on a line with the doors of the several *Mandapams.* On the south of the southern parapet wall are the *Madappaly,* (a room where rice, cake etc. are prepared for the *pooja*), the *Vahanasalai* (a hall for keeping vehicles called *vahanam*) and the *Kalanchiam* (a store room).

To the north is a small room called *Vasanthaman-dapam* where the *image* is first brought before it is taken in procession on festival days. To the East is a very small room called *yakam* where over a fire called *omam* the *diety* is invoked on such days.

The Vaddukkoddai Church was built by the Dutch in 1678 in the time of the Dutch Governor Pyl and is about the largest church in the Peninsula if not in the Island. The pillars and walls are very massive. About one fourth of the premises is used for the Vaddukkoddai High School.

The Reclamation Road enclosing the fore shore (about 78 acres in extent) between the Jaffna customs and the Provincial Engineer's office was started as a relief work by Sir William Gregory in the year 1877 when, in addition to a severe outbreak of cholera, there was great distress in the place. This wall was torn up to the foundation in many places by the severe cyclone in 1884. It was again very substantially built by prison labour under the supervision of Sir Wm. Twynam. It is imperative on sanitary grounds and as a means of relieving the terrible congestion at Karayoor to fill up the enclosed area. With the railway running by its side this work should not be delayed.

The Punnalai Causeway affording great convenience to people travelling between Jaffna and Kaits is a neat piece of work stretching across the sea for a distance of two miles. The original causeway was washed away by the cyclone of 1884.

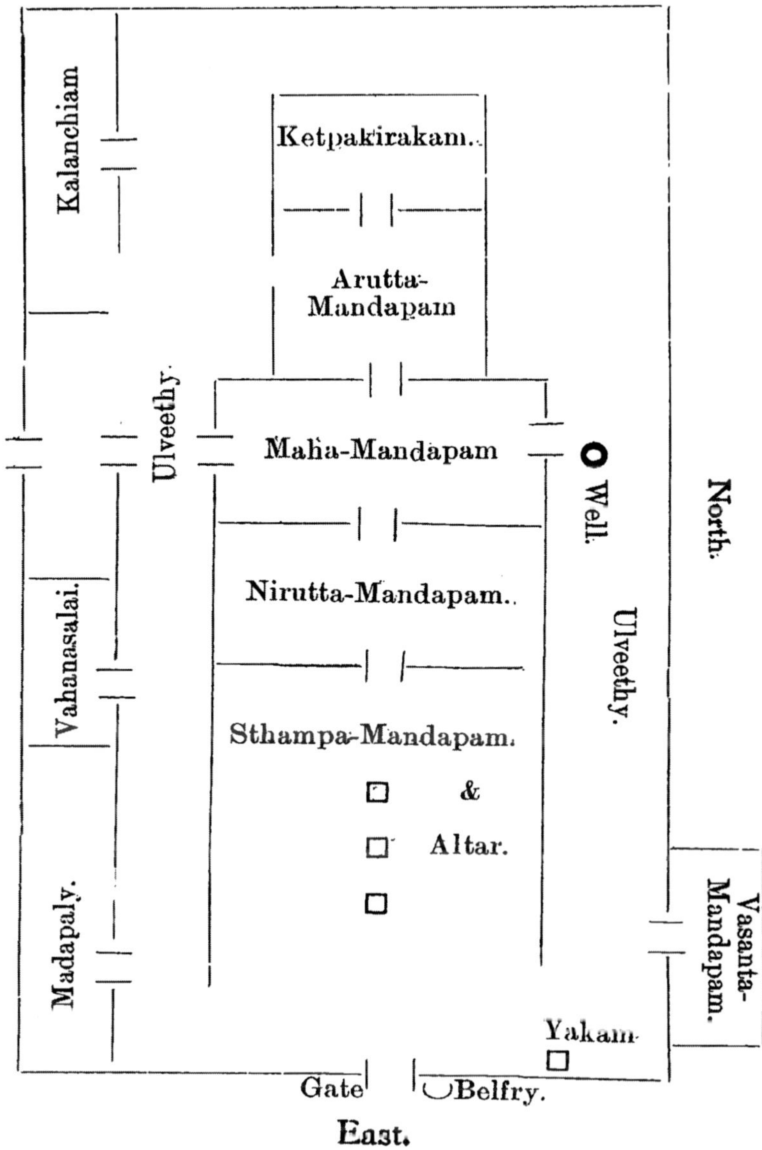

The Ground Plan of a Hindu Temple.

Chapter X.

PRINCIPAL ROADS WITH THEIR DISTANCES, NOTING PLACES OF INTEREST.

No. 1. JAFFNA TO ELEPHANT PASS.

Starting at the Jaffna Fort and going eastward we pass through the Esplanade leaving the Police Station on the right sheltered under some banian trees. Reluctantly emerging from the fine scenery of the Esplanade we take the Main Street, meeting the Rest House on the right and the Courts and the Land Registry buildings on the left. The Main Street presents a view of the old Dutch habitations now used as shops and dwelling houses. Within a mile from the Fort on the left and just before the Railway level-crossing there is a Roman Catholic Convent. A little further up we meet the cross road leading to St. Patrick's College, a Roman Catholic Cathedral and Bishop's quarters. Proceeding further and leaving St. John's College and St. John's Church with its slate covered roof on the left and making a turn to the left (a minor road) and then to the right we come to the Jaffna Kachcheri and its reputed park formed by the late Mr. Dyke. It is about 1½ miles from the Fort.

Then pressing on the same route we pass Siviyateru, Atthikado, Chemmani, Upar bridge and toll station (which is about 4 miles from Jaffna), Chavankoddai and Navatkuli (which is a railway station—

the road along the Railway line leading to Thanankilappoo through Maravanpulavu). Going at right angles to the railway line at the Navatkuly station we come to Kaithadi (6⅓ miles) meeting on the left the road from Manippai. We next reach the Nunavil junction 8¾ miles from Jaffna. The road on the left goes to Pt. Pedro 12 miles from the junction. We then get to Chavakachcheri at the 11th mile, which is provided with a Post and Telegraph Office, Minor Courts, a Rest House and a market.

Then we go to Kodigamam Railway station and market (15 miles) and leaving there the road on the right to Kachchai and the road on the left to Pt. Pedro (10½ miles from Kodigamam by Coach), we pass through Mirusuvil toll station (17 miles), Odduveli (19½ miles), Vempabikkeni and come to Palai (24 miles) where there are a Rest House, District Engineer's Office, Dispensary, Post and Telegraph office, Railway station and a lot of cocoanut estates. Within about a mile from Palai we meet on the right a large tank at Karantai. Four miles more and we are on the central road proper, leading to Vavoniya. The Elephant Pass Rest house is on the left of this road 33 miles from Jaffna; a bye-path leads to it.

NO. 2. JAFFNA TO POINT PEDRO.

From the Clock Tower on the Esplanade, leaving the Weslyan Mission houses and Central College on the left and proceeding northwards across the fields we do the first turn to the right and having had a sight of the Friend-in-need-Society Hospital on our left we take the next turn to the left and pass the Railway level-crossing. From here we proceed towards the Ariakulam tank. Passing it we take the right hand road and go to Nallore Kandaswamy temple (1¾ mile). We pass the 2nd mile post and do the turn to the left and within a 100 yards from the turn we see on our left at a short distance the Nallore C. M. S. Church in the vicinity of which is the Jumnari. Further up we meet on our right the old gateway of the palace of the Tamil King at Sangily toppu. Higher up on our left is the Chaddanatha temple. From here we proceed without much to attract our attention and pass the 4th mile post. (Just before the 4th mile is a junction of 5 roads. The one on the east goes to Erupalai; the one next to it and to the north-east is an old road meeting this main road at about 4½ miles from Jaffna; and the one on the west meets the Jaffna--Kangesanturai road at Kockuvil.)

On an eminence we find a newly erected Roman Catholic Church at Copay (4½ miles) and further on a Receiving Post Office. At the 5th mile is the Copay C. M. S. School and Church. Going northwards we soon meet the junction of the Manippay—Kaitady road from west to east. We next pass the villages of Neervali, Siruppiddy and come to Puttur (8 miles) where stands on the left of the road a Dispensary and further up at a junction of roads is a Post Office. (The road towards the east goes to Kodikamam about 8½ miles from this junction.) Higher up we come to a Govt. bungalow and a Wesleyan Church. Here a road branches off to the west and goes by the famous tidal well called *Nelavarai* in Puttur (2 miles from the junction) to Chunagam. (At the 10¾ mile a road on the left leads to Achchuveli and Tondaimanar 3½ miles from the junction.) Leading onwards we come to the Vallai bridge (12¼ miles) and the toll station. Then comes a junction of three roads 13½ miles from Jaffna.

The road on the left goes to Valvedditurai (17 miles pasing the American Mission Station at Udupitty (15¼ miles) and Valveddy (16 miles). Valveddi turai has a Post and Telegraph Office, a market and the Customs. Taking the right turn at the market we go eastward almost along the seashore and reach Point Pedro 21¾ miles from Jaffna by this cut from the Vallai junction.

We might as well take the road to the right at the Vallai junction (13½ miles from Jaffna) to go to Point Pedro passing through Karanavai (14½ milés) Nelliadi (17½ miles) and Manthigai or Puloli where we find a Govt. hospital. Point Pedro is 21 miles by this cut. Here are the Customs, the Minor Courts, a Post & Telegraph office and a market.

NO. 3. JAFFNA TO KANGASENTURAI.

Taking the westernmost road of the Esplanade leaving Muniapper Kovil on the left and the Petrolium Stores on the right, we pass along the road to the West of the Grand bazaar lined on either side with cloth shops for some distance till we reach Katiresan and Sivan temples on the left. Proceeding further we see the Hindu College on the right (1½ miles from Jaffna) now under construction. Kokkuvil where there is a stoppage of the train for the convenience of the passengers is in this road 3 miles from Jaffna. A little over 4½ miles from Jaffna on the right is the Inuvil Hospital. Then comes a junction of 4 roads, the one on the east meets the Jaffna—Point Pedro road at Kopay and passes to Kaithady; the one on the west goes to the American Mission Church and Girls' Boarding School at Uduvil and passes to Manippay. Now keeping to the main road we come to Chunagam (6 miles) with its market and an approach road to the Railway station, Then comes a junction of roads about 7½ miles from Jaffna. The road on the left takes us to the Mallakam Minor Courts soon to be abolished. Going northwards at 9½ miles we come to Tellepalai with its Normal School and Press under the American Mission on a junction of 4 roads. The road on the east takes us to the Railway level crossing where there is a stoppage of the train for the convenience of the passengers. Further north in the main road near the 10th mile is Maviddapuram with its famous Kandaswamy temple. There is a minor road towards the west branching off to Keerimalai. The main road takes us to Kangesanturai nearly 12 miles from Jaffna. There are a Post and Telegraph Office, a Rest House, the Customs and the Railway terminus.

NO. 4. JAFFNA TO KAITS.

Following the road to Kangesanturai (No. 3) up to the first turn to the left from the Hindu College we go towards the west to Oddumadam (1¾ miles) and then through the fields. Leaving the Jaffna lagoon on the left at Kallunday we come to the Valukkaiattu bridge about 5 miles from Jaffna. (We might, instead of following the Kangesanturai road go south of the Fort to Pannaiturai and thence to Kallunday.) From the Valukkaiattu bridge we take the road on the right and having left Araly at the 6th mile we go to Vaddukkodai (7 miles) with its time honoured Jaffna College and the American Mission Church originally a Dutch edifice. On the 9¼ mile begins the Punnalai causeway which extends to 2 miles till it reaches the road from Karativo. As we go a little further a road branches off to Karativo west and meets the main road at the Kaits end of Karativo (14¼ miles.) Between Karative and Kaits communication is maintained across the harbour by means of a ferry boat. At Kaits the Customs buildings, Minor Courts and the Rest House are close to each other and the landing jetty. The Post Office and the Dispensary are within ¼ and ½ a mile respectively from the jetty. Kaits or Karativo may also be reached by a boat from Jaffna, the distance being 11 miles by sea.

NO. 5. JAFFNA TO PUNNALAI *via* MANIPAY.

Getting to Oddumadam as described in No. 4 you go towards the north leaving the fields to your left, a little higher up you pass a junction. Taking the left turn and within a few hundred yards north of the fields, you see some banian trees and a raised ground along the road on the right. Thereabouts is a public cremation ground. Passing Anaicottai and Suthumalai you go to Manipay 5 miles from Jaffna. Here is the famous Maruthady Pilliar Kovil with an American Mission Church and a Hospital opposite it. As you go westward you find the Manipay Post and Telegraph Office. Close by are a burial and a cremation ground. Going southwards through a lane you come to a spot at Navaly where a deep pit was suddenly formed on the 19th May 1905 by the subsidence of the surface soil. Leaving Manipay, wend your way westward till you come to Changanai (7½ miles) where you find a market and further up the ruins of a Dutch or Portuguese Church. At the 8¼ mile is Chittankeni Pilliar Kovil at the junction of four roads. (The road on the left goes to Vaddukkoddai and Araly; the one on the left goes to Mathakal.) Going westward at about the 9½ miles you come to Chulipuram where stands the Victoria College. Passing the College and taking the next turn to the left you come to Moolai (10½ miles) and thence to Punnalai 11½ miles by this cut. The road through Vaddukkoddai is only 9¼ miles from Jaffna to Punnalai.

NO. 6. KODIGAMAM TO PT. PEDRO.

From Kodigamam Railway Station by the market and thence northwards through Varany (4 miles) we reach the Mulli toll station 6 miles from Kodigamam. 2½ miles higher up is Puloli with its hospital. And from there northwards we reach Pt. Pedro 10½ miles from Kodigamam. It is a good sea coast town noted as a resort for patients subject to pulmonary complaints.

NO. 7. PT. PEDRO TO PUNNALAI.

This route is along the sea shore. Starting at the Customs house it passes along the sea shore leaving the Rest House, the Magistrate's quarters and the Wesleyan Mission house on the left till we meet Kandavanam temple at Policandy (4 miles from Pt. Pedro) and come to Valvettiturai (5 miles.) Leaving the Customs and the market at Valvettiturai and then the Sivan temple on the left we go to Urikadu (6 miles) which is used as a sanitarium by the American Missionaries. Close by at Kerudavil (about 7 miles) is the famous cavern called *Mandapam*; and from there we go to Tondaimanar (7¾ miles) where is a toll station with a salt depot close by. We then pass Achchuvely (8 miles) and Myiliddi (13 miles) and reach Kangasenturai 14 miles from Pt. Pedro. We pass on to Keerimalai (16¼ miles) where we find the mineral springs along the sea shore. Continuing to go westward along the sea side road we reach Mathakal 19½ miles from Pt. Pedro. (A minor road on the left goes to Pandeteruppu.) We proceed and passing through Tiruvedinilai (23 miles) come to the Punnalai causeway 25¼ miles from Pt. Pedro. About midway between the 23rd and 24th miles from Pt. Pedro on the right towards the sea shore which is about a furlong from the road is the estate where we find that curious cocoanut plant referred to in the last Chapter.

Chapter XI.

TOWNS, AND VILLAGES.

The following is a complete list of the towns and villages the population of which exceeds 1,000 according to the census taken in 1901. For the sake of convenience they are arranned alphabetically with useful notes, marking the Division in which they are situated. The numbers marked against the names indicate population of the town or village. The figures with "miles" following them shew the approximate distance of the place by road (unless otherwise indicated) from the Jaffna Fort.

The local jurisdiction of the several Courts of the sula are as follows:

The District Court, Jaffna has jurisdiction over the Peninsula in all civil cases where the subject matter of the action is valued over Rs. 300 and in all criminal cases committed before it by the several minor courts.

The minor courts of Pt. Pedro and Chavagachcheri have jurisdiction over the Vadamirachi, the Tenmirachchi and the Pachchilaipaly Divisions; those of Kayts have jurisdiction over the Islands Division; those of Jaffna and Mallakam over the Jaffna the Valikamam and the Punakari divisions, but the Police Court of Jaffna has concurrent juridiction with those of Pt. Pedro, Chavagacherry, Mallakam and Kayts.

Delft is provided with a Village Tribunal to try cases involving matters of Rs. 20 and less. If over they go to the minor court at Kayts.

Alaveddy—4234—8½ miles—in Valigamam North. Oranges and plantains are grown. It is noted for its fire-works.

Alvay—5219—19 miles—in Vadamirachi West—noted for onions, chillies and jaggery.

Anaicottai — 2349—3 miles—in Valigamam West—noted for *gingilee* oil.

Analative—1543—16 miles by sea—in the Island Division— noted for chanks the number of which has now largely decreased. Cotton was largely cultivated here. It is otherwise called *Donna Clara*, a lady of that name having been the owner of this islet in the time of the Portuguese. In the charts it has been called *Rotterdam*.

Araly South—1576—6½ miles—in Valigamam West—low land where the water is brackish. So is Araly North.

Atchuvely South— 1709— 11 miles—in Valigamam East—with a small market and the ruins of a Portuguese church—noted for its breed of country dogs.

Averangal——1293—10 miles—in Valigamam East—with a small market and groves of *illuppai* trees. "A class of people, not unlike the gypsies of England, lead a strolling life and impose on the credulity of the people by telling fortunes."

Chandiruppai—2260—6¼miles—in Valigamam West.

Changanai—313—7½ miles—in Valigamam West—with a large market and the ruins of a Portuguese church. Pottery is carried on on a small scale.

Chavagachcheri—3813—11 miles—in Tenmirachchi—with a market, a Rest house, Railway station, a post and telegraph office and minor courts sitting on alternate weeks with Pt. Pedro. This name is said to be the corruption of *Javakachcheri* i. e. the village of the Javanese. It has a history of being the place where soldiers from Java were stationed.

Chiruppiddy—1586—7$\frac{3}{4}$ miles—in Valigamam East—plantains are largely grown.

Chulipuram—3809—9$\frac{1}{2}$miles—in Valigamam West with Victoria College and a receiving post office.

Chunnagam—3224—6 miles—in Valigamam North—noted for its market which supplies other markets with vegitable produce.

Chutumalai—2460—4$\frac{1}{2}$ miles—in Valigamam West—noted for its tobacco.

Colombagam has a population less than 1000 and is 3 miles from the fort, in the Jaffna Division.

Delft, Island of—3906 27 miles by sea—a division in itself. It has a separate Maniagar who is also President of the village tribunal. Casie Chitty in his Gazeteer published in 1833 says "Government till lately kept a stud, the expense of which exceeded £1000 per annum; but the horses were ill shaped and bad, consequently the establishment has been abolished." An attempt has been recently made to revive the stud but without any success.

The mail is carried twice a week by *katmaram*. The island lies in comparatively deep water which is boisterous during the south-west monsoon.

In the old charts it has been called *Itha da vacas* or the cows' Island; but its original name is *Neduntive* or the long island, which name is even now retained in Tamil. It is about 8 miles long by 3 broad and is entirely surrounded by a coral reef. The Dutch had a fort here.

Elalai—3461—7$\frac{1}{2}$ miles in Valigamam North.

Eluthumadduval in Tenmaradchi produces paddy and has a market. It was used by the Dutch to keep the elephants previous to exportation to India. It is a small village by the railway line.

Imaianan —1742—15½ miles in Vadamaradchi West. There are two villages by this name. This one is in Udup-piddy and the other is at Kaddaively about three miles from here towards Pt. Pedro.

Inuvil—1600—4½ miles in Valigamam North with a Hospital for women under the American Mission. The average number of patients treated daily is 43.

Irupalai—1193—4 miles in Valigàmam East. Pottery is carried on in a small scale.

Jaffna is the chief town of the Peninsula as well as of the Northern Province. It has a population of about 33,879 covering an area of about 7½ square miles, with about 4,517 persons to a square mile. It ranks as the third town in Ceylon the first two being Colombo (154,691) and Galle (37,165). The houses in the Pettah generally consists of a single story, many of which are large and commodious, with broad verandahs, lofty ceilings and spacious apartments. The streets are abroad, well made and regular. Sir E. Tennent says: "of all the Settlements of Holland in the Island, none is still so thoroughly Dutch in its architecture and aspect as the town of Jaffna." Burghers, the descendants of the Portuguese and of the Dutch who remained behind after the fall of their respective Governments, live mostly in the Pettah.

The Fort, the clock tower and the Reclamation road have been described elsewhere (see ch. ix). The Kachcheri is provided with a park or rather garden formed by the late Mr. Dyke but much neglected since his days. The Post and Telegraph office is close to the customs and occupies the old O B. C. buildings. Opposite to it are the offices of the Jaffna Commercial Corporation which does some banking business and of the Jaffna Steamship Coy. The Courts, the Land Registry and the Rest House face the Esplanade.

Kadduvan—1218—7½ miles in Valigamam North on the way to Palalithurai.

Kaithady—26025 miles—in Tenmaradchy close to the Navatkuly railway station.

Kaits with a population less than 1000 and at a distance of 14½ miles from Jaffna ranks the third port in Ceylon. The harbour affords safe anchorage for shipping at all seasons of the year, and is much frequented by country craft and small vessels. The entrance is not deep enough to admit larger vessels. It is part of the Island called *Leyden.*

Fort Hammenhiel (described in ch. ix.) stands in the sea about 1½ miles from the landing jetty. The ruins of Fort *Eyrie* is in the shore opposite to the Fort Hammenhiel. Places of some importance are the minor courts, the customs, the rest house, the dispensary, the post office and a few R. C. Churches. A telegraph office is about to be opened.

Kaits or Kayts derives its name from the Portuguese word *Cays* a term for a wharf. In Tamil it is called *Urkavatturai.* CasieChitty says that its Singhalese name was *Ooratotte* (or hog-ferry) which originated in a fabulous story of *Sakreya* (who was metamorphosed into an enormous hog) having swam across from the Coromandel coast and effected a landing at this place.

Kangesanturai—with a population less than 1000 is 11½ miles from Jaffna in Valigamam North. It is an open roadstead frequented however by large ships during the south-west monsoon when it becomes a busy port. There are a light-house, a dispensary, a post and telegraph office and a rest house. The foun dation of an old Dutch fort is seen close to the customs. Kangesanturai from the fact of its being now made the terminus of the Northern Railway has a great future before it.

It derives its name from Kangesan (another name for Kandaswamy) whose image was brought here from India on its way to Maviddapuram Kandaswamy-kovil.

Karadive—8850—13 miles—in the Islands Division, connected to the mainland by the Punnalai causeway. Cloth dying has long been an industry here from the presence of the *Chaya* root which Baldeus preferred to all the varieties found in India. Karadive was formerly resorted to by the ships of the Dutch East India Coy. to furnish themselves with fuel of which there was it seems a great abundance. It is also called *Amsterdam.*

Karampaikkurichchi—1021-18½miles—in Vadamirachchi East close to Kodikamam.

Karampan—2688—15 miles—in the Islands Division forming part of *Leyden* and being south of Kaits.

Karanavai—4679—16 miles—in Vadamirachchi West. Salt is naturally formed here.

Karaveddy—8995—19½miles—in Vadamirachchi West close to Pt. Pedro noted for onions, chillies and jaggery.

Katchay a small village in Pachchilaipaly division. 19 miles from Jaffna, produces paddy.

Keerimalai a small village 12 miles from Jaffna in Valigamam North noted for its fresh water springs on the sea shore.

It literally means mongoose-hill. It was so called because Nagilasamuny was miraculously delivered here of his mongoose face. Nagilasakovil named after him is here.

Klaly a small village 20 miles south-east of Jaffna.

Kockuvil—4659—3 miles—in the Jaffna Division noted for its trade in tobacco.

Kondavil—3225—3½ miles—in the Jaffna Division

Kopay -4221—5 miles—in Valigamam East with extensive paddy fields and a receiving post office. The population in 1830 was 5075. It is a C. M. S. Station. A new R. C. Church has been recently built.

Kudatthanai —1142—22½ miles —in Vadamirachy East.

Madduvil—3857—12½ miles—in Tenmirachy.

Mallagam—1770—7½ miles—in Valigamam North with a Police Court about to be abolished.

Mandaitive—1690—3 miles—by sea in the Islands Division. A healthy spot.

Manippay—3183—5 miles—in Valigamam West with a post and telegraph office. It has many Hindu temples of which the one at Marutadi attracts large numbers on the Hindu New Year and other festive days. There is a Church as well as a large Hospital belonging to the American Mission. In the adjoining field is the salt water pool recently formed by the subsidence of the soil. It is fast rising in importance and wealth.

Manthuvil—1934—13½ miles—in Tenmiradchy.

Mathakal—2896—11 miles—in Valigamam West produces grapes and abounds in coral rocks.

Maviddapuram—2133—10 miles—in Valigamam North. Here stands the famous Kandaswamy Temple which attracts many during the month of July and other festive seasons. This temple was originally built by a princess from the Coromandal coast who having been born with a horse face was so miraculously delivered of it here that the place came to be called Maviddapuram or literally the city where the horse face was got rid of.

Mayliddy—1487— 12 miles —in Valigamam North. It is now a large fishing village. There was formerly a splendid Church and parsonage house erected by the Portuguese. Yams and tobacco are grown here.

Meesalai—3219—15 miles—in Tonmiradchi—2 miles from the main road.

Mirusuvil—1066—17 miles—in Tenmaradchi.

Mohamalai a small village in Pachilaippalai division with a market.

Moolay—1323—10 miles—in Valigamam West about a mile from Punnalai.

Nainative—1318—18 miles by sea—in the Islands division. It is also called *Haarlem* with 4 miles in circumference. It was formerly inhabited by *Vellales* who during the Dutch occupation passed for Brahmins in order to escape the servitude tax levied on all other castes. Here is a small temple famed however as Nagatampiran Kovil to which pilgrims resort in large numbers annually in the Tamil month of June. Here chanks are fished.

Narantani—1695—12 miles—by Araly ferry through Velanai in the Island's division.

Navaly—2812—4½ miles—in Valigamam West.

Navatkuli—1494—4 miles—in Tenmaradchy. Paddy is largely cultivated here, and in former days there was a large store for paddy. It is now a small railway station.

Neervali—3046—6½ miles—in Valigamam East in Pt. Pedro road. Plantains are largely grown here.

Nellore—is within the gravets of Jaffna about 1½ miles from the Fort. It was the seat of the Tamil Kings, the ruins of whose Palace are still to be seen. Kandaswami Temple and Jamunary are situated here. It is a C. M. S. station close to which is a private hospital started and managed by Mr. Mailvaganam of Nayanmarkadu who combining European with native methods has been successful as a dresser and surgeon. Weaving is done here in a small scale.

Nunavill—613—9 miles—in Tenmaradchy close to Chavagachcheri. Noted for pure gingilee oil.

Palaly—1960—10 miles—via Urumpiray in Valigamam

North a fishing village.

Pallai—1246—24 miles—in Pachilaipaly division with a post and telegraph office, Railway station and District Engineer's office. The village had formerly a large Church which on account of its incursions of the Kandyans was surrounded by a high wall with port holes in the nature of a redoubt. The forest now converted into coconut estates produced the wood called *jaggers'* wood which Baldeus says formed an article of export to the Coromandel coast during the Dutch period. Pallai means a den.

Pandaiteruppu—a small village 9 miles in Valigamam West. It formerly had a magnificient Church and a house adjoining, built on arches with two spacious rooms, gallery, fine gardens and a fish pond. The American Mission had, with permission, repaired the Church and dwelling house and made it one of their stations in the District. No Missionaries stay here now.

Pattaimeny—1267—12 miles—in Valigamam East north of Atchuvely.

Periavilan—1121—10 miles—in Valigamam· North about three miles from Tellippalai on the Pandaiteruppu road.

Point Pedro—1121—10 miles—in Vadamaradchy West. It is called in Tamil *Paruttitturai* or cotton harbour from the fact of the great quantity of cotton formerly produced and exported. The Portuguese called it *Puntas das Pedras* or the rocky point. It is the station of a Magistrate and of a sub-collector and is provided with a post and telegraph office, a dispensary, a market, a rest house and Roman Catholic and Protestant Churches and schools. It stands next to Jaffna as town and is now brought under the operations of the small Towns Ordinance. It is frequented as a health resort during the north-east monsoon. It trades largely with South India. It is an open roadstead. The Hindu temple with its tank in the town is on a scale "that attests the wealth and liberality of its devotees."

Polikandy—1239—18 miles—in Vadamaradchy West close to Pt. Pedro with a Pillaiyar temple of some fame.

Puloly—7386—20 miles—in Vadamaradchy West close to Pt. Pedro with a Civil Hospital.

Punkudutive—3193—12 miles—by sea in the Islands division, called *Middleburg* by the Dutch about 10 miles in circumference. Fish, oyster and chanks are plentiful along the coasts. Goats abound in the Island.

Punnalaikkadduvan—1251—10 miles—in Valigamam North.

Puttur—3503—11 miles—in Valikamam East noted for the famous tidal well.

Sarasalai—1936—12 miles—in Tenmiradchi.

Saravanai—1443—16 miles—in the Islands Division.

Siruvilan—1708—11 miles—in Valikamam North.

Tanakarakurichchi—3,098—14 miles—in Vadamiradchi West. It lies to the North of the Vallai plains (formerly scene of dacoity) on the way to Pt. Pedro.

Tavady—1,506—4 miles—in Jaffna Division noted for its country tobacco.

Tellippalai—7514—9 miles—in Valigamam North Here the train stops at the level—crossing taking and dropping passengers. Here is also a Normal School and Press under the American Mission. It may have probably gotten its name from *Telluppalai*, a stage where palanquin bearers change.

Thampalai—2,256—13 miles—in Valigamam East.

Thavalai Iyatalai—1,119—25 miles—in Pachchilaipali Division.

Thirunelvely East—1,384—3 miles—in Jaffna Division. A well to supply the town with water was tested here but the trial stopped at the well.

Tholpuram –2,181–9 miles–in Valigamam West—literally old city formerly the seat of several chieftains of the District. Its ancient glory seems to have passed away.

Thondaimanar—a small village—13½ miles—in Vadamirachi West—a toll station, derives its name King Thondaimam who with permission cut a canal to take salt from Karanavai Vellaiparavai.

Thunnalai—3,356—20 miles—in Vadamirachi West. Pottery is carried on in a small scale.

Uduppitty—a small village—15 miles—in Vadamirachi West. An American Mission Station with a Girls' Boarding School which has now been amalgamated with the one at Uduvil. Pottery is carried on in a small scale. Thoro is also a big parish by this name.

Uduvil.—2,981—5½ miles—in Valikamam North—chiefly noted as an American Mission Station with a large Girls' Boarding School (220 girls enrolled).

Urumpiray.—2474—5 miles—in Valigamam East-there are a few small unlicensed arrack distilleries which the authorities have often failed to trace.

Vaddukkoddai—7,244—7 miles--in Valigamam West with the chief station of the Americar Mission, a College and a High School. It has also a Post Office. A Telegraph Office is about to be opened.

Valvettiturai.—2,856—17 miles — in Vadamiradchi West. It has a Post and Telegraph Office,a Customs Office and a Market. Small native vessels are built here. Sir Emerson Tennent says that he saw here "a vessel of considerable tonnage on the stocks, the Tamil shipbuilders of this little place being amongst the most successful in Ceylon." It has been brought under the operations of the Small Towns ordinance.

Valvetty.—1047—16 miles—in Vadamiradchi West—within half a mile of Valvettiturai.

Vannarponne is the largest and most populous part of the town with numerous botiques, stores and the largest market in the Province called the grand bazzar in Tamil *Periakadai*.

Varany North—1,054—20 miles—in Vadamiradchi East on the Kodikamam Pt. Pedro road. Certain Tillainatha Thampiran of Varany is said to have cured the Tanjore Maharaja of his illness and got in return temples and lands in Vetharanium, South India. There are in this village many of his legal heirs who enjoy the income of those temples and lands

Vasavilan.—1,325—11 miles—in Valikamam North.

Veemankamam—1,393—9½ miles—in Valikamam North.

Velanai.—3,846—9½ miles—*via* Araly ferry. The ruins of a Dutch or Portuguese tower are seen here.

Chapter XII.

PUBLIC INSTITUTIONS AND OFFICES.

POST AND TELEGRAPH OFFICES.

We have two telegraph lines from Colombo. One comes from Colombo *via* Kandy, Matale, Anuradhapura, Vavonia and Elephant Pass to Jaffna; the other *via* Negombo, Puttalam, Mannar, Parantan junction and Elephant Pass to Jaffna. Anuradhapura and Mannar are also directly connected by a telegraph line.

Our mail from Colombo is carried by train to Anuradhapura and thence by a bullock coach (which will be displaced by the time this handbook is out) to Pallai and from there by train to Jaffna.

The following are the Post offices where we have telegraph offices as well:—

The Jaffna Post & Telegraph Office. The Post and Telegraph Master here whose fixed pay* is Rs 2.000 a year, has the immediate supervision of all the post and telegraph offices in the Peninsula. He is assisted by a deputy and a number of signallers clerks and peons.

Manipay Post & Telegraph Office. The Post Master is assisted by a signaller. It is about 5 miles from the Jaffna P. O.—coach service.

Kangesanturai Post & Telegraph Office. The Post Master is assisted by a signaller. It is about 11½ miles from the Jaffna P. O.—train service.

---

* The present Post Master gets Rs. 2,680 a year.

Valvettiturai Post & Telegraph Office. The Post Master is assisted by a signaller. It is about 16½ miles from the Jaffna P. O.—train to Kodigamam, and coach from there *via* Pt. Pedro.

Point Pedro Post & Telegraph Office. The Post Master has two assistants. It is about 21 miles from the Jaffna P. O.—train to Kodigamam and coach from there.

Chavagachery Post Office. The Railway telegraph office is utilised in sending messages handed over at the Post office. It is about 11 miles from the Jaffna P. O.—train service.

Pallai Post Office. Same as Chavagachery P. O. It is about 24 miles from the Jaffna P. O.—train service.

The following Post Offices have no telegraph offices.

Kaits Post Office, 14½ miles from the Jaffna P. O. —coach to Vaddukkoddai and thence a runner. Telegraph line has been undertaken.

Vaddukkoddai Post Office, 7 miles from the Jaffna P. O.—coach service. Telegraph line has been under taken.

Puttur Post Office, 9 miles from the Jaffna on the Pt. Pedro Road—runner service.

Vannarpornai Post Office, 2 miles from the Jaffna P. O. on the Kangesanturai Road. The coach to Vaddukkoddai takes the mails.

Jaffna Kachcheri Post Office, about 1¼ miles from the Jaffna P. O.—coach service.

Besides the above we have the following receiving post offices i. e. offices where no money orders can be cashed nor letters registered.

Chulipuram—10 miles from the Jaffna P. O. near Victoria College—runner service from Vaddukkoddai.

Mallakam—7½ miles from the Jaffna P. O.,—runner service.

Kopay, 4½ miles from the Jaffna P. O. little further away from the newly built R. C. Church — runner service.

HOSPITALS.

Friend-in-need-Society Hospital, the oldest hospital in Jaffna, is situated to the north of the Esplanade and is managed by a lay committee. It receives a Government subsidy of Rs. 8,000 a year.

Inuvil Hospital for females and children is managed by the American Mission. It is 4½ miles from Jaffna on the Kangesanturai road.

Puloly Civil Hospital under Government is at Puloly about two miles from Pt. Pedro.

Manipay Hospital under the American Mission is situated at Manipay, 5 miles from Jaffna.

Infectious Hospitals. There are also two infectious hospitals, one behind the Jaffna Fort and the other at Kangesanturai.

OUT—DOOR DISPENSARIES.

There are out-door dispensaries at the following places. The numbers marked against them denote their distances from the Jaffna town.

Chavagachcheri	11	Pt. Pedro	21
Chempianpattu	28	Punkudutivu	12
Delft	27	Puttur	9
Jaffna Town	—	Vaddukkoddai	7
Kaits	14½	Valvettiturai	17
Kangesanturai	12	Vannarponnai	1½
Nainativu	18	Varany	20
Pallai	24		

REST HOUSES.

Jaffna Rest house is at the base of the Main Street where it starts from the Esplanade.

Kaits Rest house is within 100 yards from the Kaits jetty and is $14\frac{1}{2}$ miles from Jaffna.

Kangesanturai Rest house is behind the Railway Station and $11\frac{1}{2}$ miles from Jaffna.

Point Pedro Rest house is by the sea side close to the customs and 21 miles from Jaffna.

Chavagachcheri Rest house is within 100 yards from the Railway Station and is 11 miles from Jaffna.

Pallai Rest house is close to the Railway station and is 24 miles from Jaffna.

Elephant Pass Rest house is on the Central Road facing the lagoon where the water does not dry up, 33 miles from Jaffna; a bye-path leads to it.

Pass Beshuter Rest house is on the road to Mullaitive north-east to Elephant Pass 34 miles from Jaffna.

Chundiculam Rest house on the Mullaitive road about 45 miles from Jaffna. It is on the south-eastern arm of the Peninsula.

LIBRARIES AND READING ROOMS.

Jaffna Public Library opposite the Jaffna Rest house receives a Government subsidy of Rs. 200 a year. There are about 92 members on the roll.

St. Joseph's Catholic Library on the Main St. Jaffna is under the Roman Catholic Mission.

Victoria Reading Hall was started in commemoration of the golden jubilee of our late Queen Victoria.

Pt. Pedro Reading Room is at Pt. Pedro 21 miles from Jaffna.

Y. M. C. A. Reading Room is at Main St. Jaffna.

CIVIL SERVICE.

The Government Agent belongs to the 1st class of the civil service receiving a salary of Rs. 16,000 rising to Rs. 18,000 a year, by annual increments of Rs. 500. The Government Agents of the Western and Central Provinces belong to this class. We hope that with the opening of the Railway to the North, our Government Agent will be given a seat in the Legislative Council.

The District Judge belongs to the 2nd class of the Civil Service with a salary of Rs. 10,000 rising to Rs. 12,0C0 by annual increments of Rs. 500, after three years in that class.

The Police Magistrate of Jaffna and Mallakam belongs to the 4th class drawing a salary of Rs. 5,000 a year.

The Police Magistrates at Pt. Pedro (and Chavagachery) and Kayts. and the Office Assistant to the Govt. Agent are in the 5th class drawing salaries of Rs. 4000 a year.

N.B. The Governor has power to interchange officers of the 2nd and 3rd classes *inter sed*, and officers of the 4th and 5th classes *inter se*.

The Provincial Engineer draws a salary of Rs. 6,500 rising to Rs. 8,000 by increments of Rs. 500 after the 2nd year.

Two District Engineers draw salaries of Rs. 3,000 and Rs. 4,000 each.

JUSTICES OF THE PEACE.

The Govt. Agent is a Justice of the Peace for the Island.

The following are the J. P.'s for the Northern Province.

Mr. T. M. Tampoe, Proctor and Notary.

Mr. T. C. Changarapillai, Crown Proctor & Notary.

Mr. V. Tambipillai, Deputy Fiscal.

Mr. R. H. Lembruggen, retired Inspector of Schools.

Mr. A. Mailvaganam, Unofficial Police Magistrate as well—Kopay.

The District Judge, Police Magistrates and Superintendent of Police are *ex officio* J. P.'s for their districts and divisions.

MANIAGARS.

Each division* of the Jaffna District has a Maniagar. The Maniagars of Jaffna, Valigamams Vadamirachchi West and Tenmirachi draw salaries from Rs. 800 rising to Rs. 1,100 by annual increments of Rs 50 a year. The Maniagars of the other divisions draw from Rs. 500 rising to Rs. 700 by annnal increments of Rs. 50 a year.

The **Provincial and District Road Committee** manages the Minor roads of the Peninsula.

---

* See chapter I.

Chapter XIII.

THE FAUNA OF JAFFNA.

The Fauna of Jaffna is comparatively limited owing to the sandy nature of the soil, the want of forests of any size and the shallowness of surrounding sea.

The following is an alphabetical list of the animals, birds and insects common in the Peninsula.

Ants. There are several varieties of them. White ants or *termes* are a variety of them. They are mostly found in spots where the climate is not chilly or the soil too sandy. These insects are most destructive to trees, plants, wood-work of houses etc. Ebony and iron-wood are too hard for their operations Woodwork impregnated with camphor or aromatic are preserved from their work.

Bats live in the roofs of bungalows and the ruins of every building. They suspend themselves hanging by the claws of the hind-legs, pressing the chin against the breast. They move about in the nights in search of prey.

Bees are not reared here as in other countries. They form their honey in the hollows or on the branches of trees.

Buffaloes are largely found in the eastern part of the Peninsula. There are no wild buffaloes in Jaffna.

Butterflies are common during the dewy season i. e. from December to February.

Chameleon. Sir E. Tennent says that the true chameleon is formed in Jaffna where it frequents the trees in slow pursuit of its insect prey. The abililty of this creature to turn all the colours of the rainbow has attracted the notice of all ages. It is becoming very rare now.

Chanks are fished in the seas of Analaitive and Punkudutive.

Cobra de Capello is venomous enough to inflict a fatal wound.

Cows are very small in size and the milk they give is comparatively little. The pastures are few.

Crocodiles live exclusively in fresh water tanks. When there is no rain they bury themselves in the mud and lie in a state of torpor till released by the recurrence of the rain.

Crows are glossy black. They frequent houses and are common all over the Island. Experiments were tried by taking them to the Estates in the Straits Settlements for picking out insects. They soon came about the houses leaving the Estates.

Deer are reared and domesticated. Wild ones are few.

Dogs. Sir E. Tennent says: "There is no native wild dog in Ceylon, but every village and town is haunted by mongrels of European descent, which are known by the generic description of *Pariahs.*" They live on almost anything even on fruits. They serve the purpose much better than the high class dogs newly imported. For fear of their becoming rabbid many of the stray ones are killed in the month of February or March. There is now a tax of 25 cts.

Dragon flies with their gauzy wings are eminently beautiful and come during the winter season.

Dugongs appear in the lagoons during the south-west monsoon.

Fleas are a pest. Mud floors and dust breed them. Besmearing the floors with cow-dung drives them away for the time being.

Frogs frequent wells.

Geekoes (lizard) chirp *chic, chi , chit* on search of prey. It has the faculty of dropping the tail when it wishes to escape from an enemy.

Hares are common in the Islands Division.

Hawks and **Kites** carry away chickens.

Horses of good breed are rare. The Delft ponies are notorious for their backing and do not find a local market. South Indian horses find some favour owing to their cheapness. Australian hoises and cobs are now on the increase

Jackals.

Leeches.

Mongoose.

Monkeys are becoming rare.

Mosquitoes are very common during the winter season.

Oxen are largely brought from South India. The local ones are of a very small size.

Owls belong to a vulture class and are well known by the hideous noise they make at nights.

Parrots.

Pigeons and **doves.**

Rats.

Rat Snakes are rarely killed. They are not very harmful.

Scavenger beetles are to be seen wherever the presence of putrescent and offensive matter affords opportunity to sever it into lumps proportionate to their strength: they roll it along in search of some place sufficiently soft in which to bury it.

Terrapins are usually kept alive in wells to clear impurities.

Tics annoy cattle and dogs.

Turtles are edible and are found in the adjoining seas. They are poisonous at certain seasons. The hawksbill turtle which supplies the tortoise shell of commerce is not found here.

Wasps build their nests on the rafters of the roofs of houses and on trees.

Chapter XIV.

CASTE.*

The able reporter on the census of 1901 writes: "Caste cannot be abolished; it is too much ingrained in human nature and in the oriental nature. It is not an affair of religion. The adoption of Christianity makes little difference: Christians in Ceylon are among the greatest sticklers for caste. Its badges of *connubium* (intermarriage) and commensality (eating together) are matters of private concern, with which a government cannot interfere."

The Tamils are, like Romans of old, a "nation of yeomen" and like them hold agriculture in the highest esteem. "The world wheels behind the ploughs," says the Tamil sage *Tiruvalluvar;* "of all work, therefore, ploughing is chief." In this race of farmers three families appear to have early attained to a predominent position, and they founded the famous *Pandya*, *Chola* and *Chera* dynasties from whom we have had our kings.

The Portuguese historian of India, F. Sousa, writing of the social divisions of his time (17th century) says: "the most renowned families are the *Rajas*, an ingenious people who would rather lose their lives than their arms in battle; and the Brahmins who contend with the *Rajas* for precedence. The Chetties (not the

* The term Caste, which is the Portuguese *casta* from Latin *castus*, means breed or race and was first used by the Portuguese for the Social divisions of the Hindus. The Sanscrit term is *Varna*, colour.

present Nattuccotta Chetties) are the richest merchants. The *Vellales* or the country people are held in such esteem that kings marry their daughters to them.

Again writes the able reporter, "There are two main divisions of the *Vellales* from early times: those who themselves cultivated lands, and those who had them cultivated. There was another division into merchants, titled *Vellales* and other *Vellales*. Together with priests, and the kings they constituted the aristoracy of the land. The order assigned to the merchants indicates the advance of commerce or of Aryan ideas, according to which the *Vaisya* held the third place. Under the head of each family lived in dependent freedom, analogus to the relation of client to patrician in ancient Rome or of vassal to lord in the feudal times in Europe, classes who performed personal and domestic services and laboured for their chief in industrial and other occupations were called *Kudimakkal*. The chief was entitled to the service of the feudatory whenever required and the latter to a share of the produce of land cultivated, to perquisities at weddings, funerals, etc. These classes were the washerman, barber, potter, gold or silversmith, brazier, mason, blacksmith, carpenter, oilmonger, salt dealer, betel seller, garland maker, grave digger, chank blower, fisher, tailor, etc." including some classes which were slaves.*

Mr. Simon Casie Chitty in his appendix to Ceylon Gazetteer published in 1833 says: "The *Tamuls* (or as commonly though improperly denominated by Europeans, *Malabars*) are according to the institutions of

* It may be noted with satisfaction that slavery was in 1844, extinguished without a claim for compensation. The slaves were employed as labourers in the fields and gardens.

the country, divided into four principal *varna* or tribes. The first is called *Pirama*, the second *Katrya*, the third *Vaisya*, and the fourth *Sutra*.

"I. The Pramaners can alone officiate in the priest hood, like the Levites among the Hebrews.

The *Piramaner* subdivide themselves into a variety of small *gotras* or tribes, denominated after the patronymics of their respective founders or the particular mode of worship followed by them. The following is a catalogue of the several sub-divisions of the *Piramaner*, 1. *Vadamer*, 2. *Kodi Vadamer*, 3. *Vadatisa Vadamer*, 4. *Cholatisa Vadamer*, 5. *Paratama shaki*, 6. *Emmayirattar*, 7. *Kanmayirattar*, 8. *Muvayirattar*, 9. *Vilyer*, 10. *Muk'kaniyer*, 11. *Varattumer* 12. *Saneyer*, 13. *Patter*, 14. *Sholiyer*, 15. *Kandramanikkam*, 16. *Alaker*, 17. *Vrahacharaman*, 18. *Suther*, 19. *Purokitha Piramanar*, 20. *Avideyer*, 21. *Kaniyaler*, 22. *Poser*, 23. *Punenul kanakker*, 24. *Kundukoleger*.

II. "The Katriyas constitute the royal tribe of warriors. . . . They divided themselves into three distinct branches or stocks, of which the first assumed the title of *Sheren*, the second that of *Sholen*, and the third that of *Pandiyan* and they reigned separately over three independent kingdoms. . . The *Singhalese*, though forming a distinct nation, and differing in their religion, language and manners from the *Tamils*, had no kings of their own race but of the latter; and according to Lord Valentia and Mr. Joinville, 'a *Singhalese* cannot be king of *Ceylon*; that is, every person born of a *Singhalese* father or mother, is excluded from the throne.'

"The *Chakaravatis* or Kings of *Jaffna* were also *Katriyas* sprung from the stock of *Sholer* by a *Piramen* woman, of *Manavey* in *Ramanat'hapuram* and hence they took upon themselves the ambiguous title of *A'riya Vumsam* to signify both sides of their parentage, for the *Ariyer* is applied in *Tamil* equally as an epithet to the *Piramaner* as to the *Sholen*."

"III. The *Vaisyas* compose the nobility of the land, and according to the classification made by the Rev. Father J. Beschi on the authority of Vira Mandalavan* and other ancient lexicographers, they are divided into three distinct tribes or castes: viz. 1. *Tana Vaisyas* or merchants, 2. *Pu Vaisyas* or husbandmen, 3. *Ko Vaisyas* or herdsmen.

"The *Tana Vaisyas* are commonly called Chetties (not Natukotta Chetties) and the following are the names of the various small tribes into which they are subdivided: 1. *Chetties*, 2. *Velan Chetties*, 3. *Kavery Chetties*, 4. *Komely Chetties*, 5. *Pattunulkara Chetties*, 6. *Sittaktu Chetties*. 7. *Sholapuratu Chetties*.

"The *Pu Vaisyas* are commonly called *Velaler* from the *Velame* or cultivation, in which they are occupied: and the names of the subdivisions of this tribe are as follows:

1. *Karakatu velaler*. 2. *Choliya velaler*. 3. *Kodikal velaler*. 4. *Tuluva velaler*. 5. *Pandarattar*. 6. *Nynar*. 7. *Udyar*. 8. *Kontaha velaler*. 9. *Savala velaler*. 10. *Retti*. 11. *Natampadi*. 12. *Agambadiyar*. 13. *Marver*. 14. *Kaller*. 15. *Palli*.

"The *Ko vaisyas* are commonly called *Idayer* and they divided themselves into only three classes:

1, *Maleia Idayer*. 2. *Valei Idayer*. 3. *Chivizar Idayer*.

---

* There are two editions of Mandalavans *Sudamany Nikandu*. The old Manipay edition has the sub-divisions of *Vaisya* as given by Mr. Casie Chitty. But the original and the recent edition by Arumuganavaler have none of that kind.

"IV The *Sutras*, on whom devolve all the lower offices are bound to serve the preceeding three classes of *Vaisyas* during their public ceremonies, whether of a joyful or mournful nature.

"Before I proceed to give a list of the several sub-divisions or classes of the *Sutras*, I have to observe that on examination many of these classes appear to have originated from the intermarriages of the original tribes, time beyond memory, and were divided into separate castes progressively. The particulars are enumerated and recorded in *Satipedanul, D'harmapurana, Jatimala Sut'ha sangita*, and other works;

"The Sutras are distinguished by Mr. Melho into two separate branches or orders, the one including all the tribes of domestic servants, *kudimakkel*; and the other all the tribes of town servants.

"The domestic servants are eighteen in number, and are arranged as follows:

1. *Navider*, barbers.
2. *Oacher*, heralds who announce weddings and deaths.
3. *Koller*, blacksmiths.
4. *Tattar*, goldsmiths.
5. *Kannar*, brass founders.
6. *Tatcher*, carpenters.
7. *Sipper*, masons.

(3–7) These five classes are commonly denominated *kammaller* i. e. craftsmen, and have the title *assary* annexed to their proper names.

8. *Valayer*, game keepers.
9. *Paner*, tailors.
10. *Ckeku vaniyer*, oil makers.
11. *Elai vaniyer*, betel venders.
12. *Chun'ambu vaniyer*, lime burners.
13. *Kavelpulli*, watchmen.
14. *Pumalakarer*, those who sell garlands of flowers.
15. *Vettiyan*, those who burn dead bodies.

16. *Kusavar*, potters.
17. *Virakudiyan*, those who blow *chanks*.
18. *Vannar*, washermen.

"The town servants are in order as follows:

1. *Salupper*, woolen drapers.
2. *Paravas**
3. *Kareiyas*
4. *Pattanever*
5. *Pollivili*
6. *Sempadaver*
7. *Timiler*
8. *Mukiar*
9. *Paramber*.

(2–9) The different tribes of fishers and boatmen, and which are commonly called *kurukulam*; that is, the progeny of the planet *kuru* or Jupiter.

10. *Vader*, huntsmen.
11. *Muchchiyer*, painters.
12. *Kuraver*, basket makers.
13. *Iruler*, woodmen.
14. *Aripper*, sifters.
15. *Ureikarer*, scabbard makers.
16. *Maruttuvar*, medical practitioners.
17. *Tather*, stage players.
18. *Kalayer*, rope dancers.
19. *Ondipili*, snake dancers.
20. *Yalpaner*, lyrists (now called Nadduvar.)
21. *Parikulattar*, horse grooms.
22. *Tanakarer*
23. *Mavuttar*

(22–23) Elephant keepers.

24. *Chandar*
25. *Kadeyer*
26. *Nalawer*†

(24–26) The different tribes of people employed in distilling toddy and in manufacturing coarse sugar.

"* The Paravas are divided into thirteen classes very little differing from each other. The first class—chiefly headmen who bear the title of "Don" granted to them from Portugal and are distinguished from the rest by wearing a gold chain and cross about their neck. . . . . .

† "Nalavers.—*Nampis* were the swordsmen of the Wannias; when they were out of work they learnt climbing under *chanars* (climbers) and hence lost their original caste and came to be called Nalavers. (Naluvu=slip.)

27. *Eeluver,* arrack distillers or brewers.
28. *Chayekarer*, dyers.
29. *Upparaver* } Pond diggers.
30. *Otter*
31. *Uppalaver*, salt makers.
32. *Seder* } The different tribes of weavers, including lower and higher orders.
33. *Seniyer*
34. *Koliyer*
35. *Kaikoler*
36. *Saliyer*
37. *Koviyer*,* slaves of the higher order.
38. *Maraver*, makers of dry measures.
39. *Paivaniyer*, mat makers.
40. *Chiviyar*, palanquin bearers.
41. *Valluver*, soothsayers.
42. *Chakiliyer* } Shoe makers.
43. *Semmar*
44. *Parrayer*, tom-tom beaters.
45. *Paller*,† ploughmen of the lower order."

The Aryan terms "Vaisya" and "Sudra" are quite inappropriate to the classes of people designated in Mr. Casie Chitty's classification. He was probably following Manu, the Aryan law giver and other writers who followed Manu in their divisions of castes in South India and Ceylon. Even the best of Vellales‡

* Some poor vellales offerred to be slaves of temples (*Kovils*). They were called Kovilars, later on Kovyars. They are no more slaves.

† Pallars came from Chola country and learned the occupation of chanars namely, climbing. They are no more ploughmen.

‡ However there are other Vellales who call themselves "Pu Vaisyas" taking their stand on a poetical dictionary called *Sudamany Nikandu* published at Manipay. Yet the *Nikandu* has for its authority *Tivakaram* and *Pinkalantai* in both of which we find that the Vellales are called Sudras. In the correct edition of the *Nikandu* by ArumugaNavaler, the 26th Stanza of Pt. ii. says that the Vellalos come under Sudra: The 33rd *Suttram* of the 2nd part of *Tivakaram* confirms it also.

whom Mr. Casie Chitty calls "Pu Vaisya" calls himself "Sudra." Bishop Caldwell explains the situation by shewing the difference between the Aryan "Sudra" and the Dravidian "Sudra".

He says "The Brahmins who settled amongst the Dravidians and formed into castes, in imitation of the castes of the North (India) seem never at any time to have given the Dravidians—with the exception perhaps of the royal houses—a higher title than that of "Sudra." They might have styled the agricultural classes *Vaisyas* and reserved the name of *Sudra* for the village servants and the unenslaved low castes, but acting apparently on the principle that none ought to be called either Kshattriyas or Vaisyas but Ariyans, and that the Dravidians were not Aryans, they seem always to have called them Sudras however respectable their position.

"In consequence of this the title *Sudra* conveys a higher meaning in Southern than in Northern India. The primitive Sudras of Northern India seem to have been slaves to their Ayans, or in a condition but little superior to that of slaves. They seem to have had no property of their own, and can scarcely be said to have had any civil rights. In Southern India on the contrary it was upon the middle and higher classes of the Dravedians that the title of Sudra, was conferred; and the classes that appeared to be analogous to the servile Sudras of Northern India were not called Sudras, but Pallas, Paraias, &c, names which they still retain. The application of the term, Sudra, to the ancient Dravedian chieftains, soldiers and cultivators does not prove that they had ever been reduced by the Brahmins to a dependent position, or that they ever were slaves—as the northern Sudras appear to have been to any class of Aryans. The Brahmins who came in 'peaceably' and obtained the Kingdom by flatteries, may probably have pursuaded the Dravidians that in calling them Sudras they were conferring upon them a title of honour. If so their policy was perfectly successful, for the title of Sudra has never been resented by the Dravidian castes, and hence whilst in Northern India the Sudra is supposed to be a low caste man, in Southern India he generally ranks next to the Brahmin. The term 'Sudra', however is really as we have seen, as inappropriate to any class of Dravadians as the term 'Kshathriya' or 'Vaisya,' It is better to designate each Dravidian caste simply by its own name as Vellales, Nayakkas &c in accordance with the usage prevailing amongst the people themselves in each locality without attempting to classifiy the various castes according to Manu's principle of classification which in reality are quite inapplicable to them, if not indeed, equally inapplicable to the castes now existing in the North [India]."

Chapter XV.

LOCAL CUSTOMS* AND GAMES.

An exhaustive account of the social customs and manners of the Jaffnese will be impossible in this little handbook however much outsiders desire such an account. The celebration as well of marriage as of funeral rites is a matter of great importance with the Tamils who lavish large sums on such occasions. Besides these two particular rites, they have several lessor ones which are characterised by the same minuteness and ostentatious display.

MARRIAGE.

Marriage in Tamil is called *Vivagam* or *Kaliyanam.* Proposals are usually made by the elders of the parties wishing to be married. Now when a marriage proposal is made between two persons the parties of both sides exchange visits for reconnoitering and finding the true bearings of each. If the propcsal is not broken after the preliminary, a further advance is made by exchanging marriage presents. Horoscopes are consulted. The dowry question now bristles up and if not satisfactorily settled results in a rupture of all relations.

When the marriage has been definitely arranged an auspicious day is fixed for its celebration. The parents or the guardians of the contracting parties having ascertained the auspicious hour, invite their friends

*The writer is largely indebted to Mr. Simon Casie Chitty for his Essay on "Ceremonies of the Tamil castes" published as an appendix to his Gazetteer.

and relations and commence erecting a *pandal* or booth in front of their dwellings. The fixing of the first pole on the north-east is accompanied by many observances. Before it is fixed in the ground it is besmeared with pulverized sandals and turmeric and the top ornamented with a number of mango leaves and pieces of silk, and when about to be put into the hole destined to receive it they throw in small bits of gold, coral, pearl, chank &c and some cocoanut milk called *Ilaneer*. The *pandal* is decorated in pure oriental style. In the centre of the bride's pandal a *Murukku* (*erythrina*) stick is fixed, called *Arasanikkal;* and near it is raised a small alter of earth, on which is placed a ball of cowdung topped with sacred *Aruku (Agrostis linearies)* grass to represent the Diety who is invoked to preside over the nuptial rites. In front of the *arsanikkal* a quadrangular pit is dug the inside of which is besmeared with cowdung for the purpose of kindling the *omam* or sacrificial fire. Brass lamps called *kuthuvilakku* and brass pots call *chempus* with water and cocoanut on the top of each are artistically spread out round the *arasanikal.*

The bridegroom partaking of a sumptuous feast with his friends sets out with them to the bride's residence amidst the strains of music and other displays such as .illuminations and fireworks. He takes with him the *Thali* or wedding ornament and the *Kurai* or wedding apparel of which a young girl is usually the bearer either in a box or a salver. The procession which according to the rank or society to which the parties belong is either on foot or in carriages with a specially decorated conveyance for the bridegroom who takes his seat with the bride's brother or her cousin. At the entrance to the bride's-pandal stands a female with a paten full of mixture of flours and ghee, consecrated by the priest, in her hands facing the bridegroom when he comes in, waving the paten and making circular motions with it from head to foot. As the bridegroom gets into the *pandal* his companion stepping forward pours water over his feet from a brass-pot kept in readiness for the purpose and receives from the bridegroom a ring in return. The bridegroom is then led up to a dais called *manaverai* erected facing the quadrangular pit already referred to.

Now the priest ignites the sacrificial fire in the pit occassionally throwing into it handful of varieties of fine grain and a number of dried sprigs of the *Al (ficus benghalansis)*, the *Arasu (ficus, relgiosa)*, the *Itti (sacried fig)*, the *Atti (ficus udambra)*, the *Ma (mango)*, the *Karunkali (ebony)*, with the *thetpa (poa cynosuroides)* grass and *naiururi (caralsabo)* herb, also letting in drops of ghee at different intervals; and reciting each time a text from the *Veda* and a series of short orisons: The bride who had previously been bathed, dressed in splendid apparel and richly adorned with jewels is ushered into the *pandal* and is made to sit by the right side of the bridegroom. Then they both go through a long train of ceremonies. They are then given away by their guardians, a custom not unlike that observed by Europeans. The priest thereupon recites as follows: " The Sun, Moon, this Fire and God are witnesses that ——, the son of ——, now gives his daughter——, as wife to ——, who is the son of——."

The *Thali* and *Kurai* are placed on a salver and are first handed round to the guest to be touched by each of them by way of imparting their blessing. After this the *Kurai* is handed over to the bride and to her chamber she retires to get herself attired. As she returns she is made to sit on the briedegroom's left, an emblem of the position of Satti. The *Thali* now passes from the priest's hands to those of the bridegroom who with a silent prayer stands up before the bride and ties it round her neck, when the musicians play on their instruments without intermission.

Next to this is performed the rite called *panigraham,* which is that of joining the hands of the two, painting a *pottu* (the likeness of the pupil of the eye) on their foreheads and making them walk round the fire three times occasionally throwing into it handfulls of paddy mixed with flowers &c as they pass.

Now the bride is made to put her right foot on the *ammi* (a granite stone for grinding curry stuffs) while the bridegroom points out to her the con-constellation, *Arunthuthi* (a star in Great Bear) as an emblem of fidelity.

When the marriage has been thus solemnised the relations and friends then pronounce a blessing on the couple. After this they are conducted into the marriage chamber and are made to formally partake of a meal (the partaking is called *puthatkalampanikirathu).* The assembly then breaks up, not however without partaking of an entertainment and taking betel and sandal.

The Christians do not observe any of the above ceremonies expect the tying of the *thali* and the handing of the *Kurai* to which they also attach considerable importance.

FUNERALS.

As soon as it is ascertained that life is extinct the relations of the deceased place the corpse with its head to the south on sacred grass called *Thetpay* (*Poa cynosuroides*). A *pandal* is erected before the house and the washerman hangs it with the white cloth. Th· mourning of the female relatives and friends is truly pathetic.

Notice, verbal or otherwise is sent round. Friends and relatives attend. When all are assembled they bring out the corpse and pour water over it, rubbing on the head some *gingilee* oil and expressed *illuppai* seeds called *arappu*. After an ablution thus preformed the body is dressed in a clean garment and decked with wreaths of fragrant flowers; the nearest relatives of the deceased placing a pi ce of muslin over the mouth of the corpse, put on it each a few grains of rice and a coin which goes to the barbei who attends the funeral.

Before removing the body from the house, the ceremony called *Chunnamidittal* is gone through. A mortar and pestle are brought efore the corpse. Five different coloured substances are thrown into the mortar and the nearest relative who is to set fire to the funeral pyre holds the pestle and as the priest sings sacred songs recounting in fervent tones the deeds of man in this world, lifts and lets it fall into the mortar at the close of every stanza.

The stretcher in which the corpse is carried is usually made of arecannut wood and decorated with paper and cloth. Of late nailing the corpse in a coffin and pla ing it in the stretcher has become the fashion. A host of friends and relatives accompany the "cortege" to the cremation ground preceeded by tom-tom beaters. The beating oi tom-tom is almost continuous from time of death until the removal of the corpse.

The fire for the funeral pyre is taken usually by the barber.

The fire is consecrated by the priest reciting the following sancrit *Sloga* :—

" Oh dread agni, giver of light,
To planets all a real delight,
Happy giver of life to growing things,
Oh servant of God in his biddings,
Means of assimilation thou,
Cause of all digestion thou,
Deign to burn this mortal remains
And raise his soul toward high domains."

When the procession reaches the appointed place, a clear spot is selected, where piling up a number of billets of wood they lay the corpse on the top. Then the closest relative goes round the corpse three times with a pot full of water. The pot and water are an emblem of body and soul. Openings are made in the pot with a knife and the water flows out. On the third round the person carrying the pot is made to stand near the head of the corpse with his back toward it. He is now made to place the sacred fire on the pyre from behind and to walk away without ever looking back. The fire in a few hours reduces the corpse to ashes.

After attending the funeral, the people as a rule take a bath and purify themselves before returning to their homes or partaking of any food; and in the observance of this particular, they resemble the Jews among whom "when a man dieth in a tent all came into the tent and all that are in the tent are considered unclean seven days."

On the 3rd day after the cremation, the nearest relatives of the deceased proceed to the cremation ground and perform the *Kadaltal* ceremony. They gather up the ashes of the funeral pyre and putting them in a vessel they go in procession to some tank, river or Sea and throw them into it.

On the 30th day after the cremation comes the ceremony of *anthiaddy* and *Kulledduppu*. It is more an occassion for feeding the poor than for performing any ceremony.

A *pandal* is erected and decorated with white cloth. Under it the priest selects a level space and forms squares on it with coloured powders. Copper vessels called *chempoo* are arranged near the squares, The priest makes an effigy of *thetpay* grass and places it on a bier of the same material. All of which being conclud-ed, a piece of brick consecrated to the deceased is brought out under a canopy accompanied by music and placed near the squares. A wooden mortar and pestle are next put at the entrance of the pandal which some relatives strike at intervals. Thê priest kindles the sacrificial fire in a manner similar to that which is practised on occasions of marriage. The effigy is burnt and the ashes gathered up and thrown into a tank after some minor ceremonies. Again the brick is conveyed likewise into a river or tank. The persons then bathe and return home where something like a feast is ready A ceremony called *chavandy* is now gone through for purifying the house. Feast and alms-giving follow.

GENERAL.

Respect to old age. Whatever may be the assembly in which the aged may be in want of a seat, the younger men consider it a pride to grant him one of prominence with a true Spartan grace. Among members of the same family a marked regard is paid to the older ones in everything. To begin with, the younger brother does not address his elder brother by name but calls him brother. In case there be many brothers a good number of qualifying adjectives are used before the word "brother"; nor are the other relatives called by their names by the younger ones. The observance of this custom is so strict that the younger brother will not sit before his elder brother, nor the son before his father. However, Western ideas seem to be weakening these obvances.

When two persons meet each other on the way, if they be equals, they pass with a mutual bowing of the head. If not equals the younger person lowers his shawl till the elder one passes him. The lowering of the shawl and doffing the hat signify the same mark of respect.

Visiting. If a person enters one's house, he pulls off his slippers or sandals or whatever he may be wearing and is allowed to retain his turban. Before entering a *pandal* on a marriage day or on some other such occasion, the slippers or sandals have to be left in the safe-keeping of some person specially kept there. Persons of rank and position not unusually take an attendant who looks after such things. Betel and arecanuts are the local counterparts of the lighter tea and the stronger drinks of the Europeans although it is a mournful fact that drinks are fast displacing the betel and arecanut.

Spitting is not allowed on the floor of the house; but in an outer corner of the is yard reserved for that purpose. Spittoons are sometimes provided for inner appartments.

Habits and tastes. The Jaffna man is a great believer in the "bath." Early in the morning he goes to the well where he takes his bath, washing his clothes which are very light consisting of a piece of cloth four yards long and a shawl about three yards long. After going through his ablutions, he shares with the other members of his family a frugal vegetarian meal. Flesh and fish are taken at other meals by non-vegetarians.

His tastes are simple in his dress as in his food and many a bitter quarrel over a tailor's bill is thus avoided.

His help-mate is a fine typical wife free from revolutionary ideas about her own rights, gentle in her speech and graceful in her habits, and in every respect fit to be the better half of the man who toils with the sweat of his brow. In the simplicity of her dress she excels all others in the world and in the opinion of many a European of high position, she,in her simplicity, possesses a grace and shows herself to advantage with the simplest and cheapest dress. She wears a short jacket and her cloth *(cheelai)* is one of about 7½ yards in length. We cannot sav the same thing about her jewelry which is neither simple nor cheap. She is of a slender build and her movements are free.

Oil bath. A word now about the oil bath which is sometimes laughed at by persons who look down upon any custom that is foreign to them and of which they are in blissful ignorance. In the tropics where the heat is intense the oil bath once a week at least becomes necessary. The writer knows of a European who takes a regular oil bath on account of its usefulness. The Olympian athletes of classic fame rubbed oil all over their body to make their limbs more supple and elastic.

Taking an oil bath has become second nature to the Jaffna man. Some even have run the gauntlet of jeers and sneers while taking oil baths in places where the foreign element was predominant. The oil used for the bath is sqeezed out of *gingilee (sesamum indica)* seed which is very widely grown here in certain seasons. In rural parts the seeds are carefully prepared for making oil in almost every house. The oil is also taken with rice. The fact that the whole process of making this oil is attended with the minutest cleanliness attests to the deal of importance that is attached to the Jaffna historical oil bath which is neglected, we are sorry to say, by a certain section of the fastidious who with a greater contempt than even a foreigner look down upon anything that is Eastern and extol the custom of the West.

THE THESAVALAMAI

or the customary law of Jaffna was promulgated by the Dutch in 1707 A. D. and was declared* by the British in 1806 to continue in full force. The law relates to civil matters such as inheritances, adoptions, gifts, purchase and sale mortgages etc.

The following is a brief sketch of the Thesavalamai. (Thesa = country, valamai = custom).

Property is divided into *modesium* or hereditary property, *cheedanam* or dowry and *Tediatetam* or acquisition.

Inheritance. The dowried daughters are not at liberty to make any further claims on the estate after the death of the parents; but should it happen that after the marriage of the daughter or daughters the parents prosper considerably, the daughters may induce their parents to increase their dowry.

If all the daughters are married and dowried "and if one or more of them dies without issue, in such case the property indisputably devolves to the other sisters, their daughters and grand-daughters; but if there should be none of them in existence, the property in such case falls in such succession to the brothers, their sons and grand-sons, if any; if not, the property reverts to the parents, if alive; and if not, the father's *modesium* or hereditary property, and the half of the *tediatetam*, or acquired property (after de-

* See Govt. Regulation No. 18 of 1806 dated 9th Dec. 1806

ducting therefrom the half of the debts), devolves first to his brother or brothers, then to their sons and grand-sons; and the mother's *cheedenam* or dowry, with the other half of the acquired property, after deducting therefrom also the remaining half of the debts, devolves to her sister or sisters, their daughters, or grand-daughters, *ad infinitum.*"

So long as there are parents the sons may not claim anything whatsoever, but on the contrary are bound to bring into the common estate all that they had earned during bachelorship. They inherit the *modesium* and are liable for the debts of their parents.

If the father dies first the mother remains in possession of the estate until the daughters marry for then she is bound to give a dowry. Sons may not demand anything while she lives, but if she marries again, the sons may demand the *modesium* and half of *thedia-thetam.* These rules *mutatis mutandis* apply to the case of the mother dying first. But if the father marries again his first mother-in-law or other nearest relatives generally take up the guardianship of the children.

Possession of Grounds and Gardens. If a co-sharer plants a particular lot in the undivided land he becomes entitled to that particular lot if that is within the extent of his share.

Mostly in Thenmaradchchy strangers are allowed to plant cocoanuts. The owner of the soil, if he supplied the plants gets two-thirds of the produce and the planter one-third; but if the planter supplied the plants he gets two-thirds of the produce and the owner one-third.

In cases of overhanging trees the fruits of the trees cultivated with trouble go to the planter, but the fruits of the other trees belong to the person whose ground they overshadow.

Otty is the mortgage of land on condition that the mortgagee should possess the same and take the profits in lieu of interest. The redemption of such lands should be after giving due notice to the mortgagee at the end of the crop. The mortgagee to get his money, must wait for one year after delivery of the land to the proprietor.

Right of Preemption is given to heirs or partners, neighbouring land owners who are also mortgagees. They are entitled to a notice of the sale.

Tharaivaram means ground duty. If a person sows the fields of another without any agreement it was deemed sufficient if the sower gives one-third of the profits to the proprietor. The present day practice varies according to circumstances.

MEASUREMENT OF SPACE.

12 Kulies=	1 Lachcham	Paddy culture
24 Lachchams=	1 Acre	
18 Kulies=	1 Lachcham	Varaku culture.
16 Lachchams=	1 Acre	

(See Blue Book 1903.)

1 Veedu or house	=24 Kulies.
1 Tottam or garden	

A *kulie* is a square "pole" (Kole in Tamil). An old Dutch pole which came under the writer's notice measured 12 ft. 4½ in. and was wasted a little at the ends. It bears the marks B. O., J. W. C., J 803.

DRY MEASURE.

32 Cut quarts=one bushel.

MEASUREMENT OF TIME.

A *Vaddum* or cycle of years consists of 60 years *each

---

*The names of the years are as follows: 1 Pirapava, 2 Vipava, 3 Sukkila, 4 Piromothutha, 5 Pirasotpatty, 6 Ankirasa, 7 Srimuka, 8 Pava, 9 Uva, 10 Tathu, 11 Esura, 12 Vekuthania, 13 Piramathy 14 Vickrama, 15 Visda, 16 Sittrapanu, 17

year with a particular name. Each year contains 365¼ days and 15 Rahai. The 12 months of the year have days each varying from 29 to 32. It does not usually happen that the number of days in a particular month this year will be the same next year. Roughly speaking the 13th of an English month is the 1st of the corresponding Tamil month. The new year is counted from Sittirai (April).

A day is divided into 60 *Nalikais.*

A *Nalikai* is divided into 60 *Venadys.*

2½ Nalikais=1 hour.

The Nalikai is counted from the dawn of the day, so that if we say it is 15 Nalikais now it means 12 o'clock noon.

7 days form a week.

Games.

Out door Games.

1. **Padyoddam.** In this game players are divided nto two sections. These sections stand in two lines about hundred yards apart from each other. A central line is also marked about 50 yards from each side. The game begins thus, say there are A B C &c. on one side on line L and X Y Z on the other side are on line N; the central line is M. A starts from L goes to M and takes in a very deep breath

---

Supanu, 18 Tharana, 19 Partipa, 20 Viya, 21 Sarvasittu, 22 Sarvathary, 23 Verothy, 24 Vekirtha, 25 Kara, 26 Nanthana, 27 Vijaya, 27 Jaya, 29 Manmatha, 30 Thurmuky, 31 Evilampy, 32 Vilamby, 33 Vekary, 34 Sarvary, 35 Pilava, 36 Supakirutu, 37 Sopakiruthu, 38 Kurothy, 39 Visuvasu, (the present year which began on the 13th April 1905). 40 Parapava, 41 Pilavanka, 42 Keelaka, 43 Kowmaya, 44 Satharana, 45 Verothikirutu, 46 Parithapy, 47 Piramathesa, 48 Ananta, 49 Iradchatha, 50 Nala, 51 Pinkala, 52 Kalayuthy, 53 Sittathy, 54 Rawittiri, 55 Thurmathy, 56 Thunthupi, 57 Rutherotekari, 58 Irathadsy, 59 Kurothana, 60 Adchaya.

and proceeds towards N, singing a song or muttering something to shew that he does not take in any more breath. He touches any one or more of the men at N, and runs back to M, muttering as he did. If he is caught by any of his opponents on the other side before crossing M, or if he stops the continual muttering before coming to M, he is out. But if he has successfully crossed M, the persons whom he had touched at N, are *out.* He returns to L, and the same is continued by both sides alternately. The side which first loses all men is the defeated party. This game, a very manly one, is now becoming obsolete owing to the dangers caused in the act of catching and wrestling in consequence. It may fairly compare with Rugby foot-ball play.

2. **The Game of Var** is a modification ot *Padyoddam.* The term of *Var* is a corruption of war perhaps. Here the middle line is not used nor is there the necessity to hold in the breath. Here the mere touch in the open field is enough; that is, the man who starts late from his line has the privilege of touching the earlier man from the other side and thus making him *out.* The men who are *out,* called *prisoners,* are put in a line at right angles three paces nearer the opponent's line. Such men may be redeemed by their own men coming and touching them without getting out. The side that wins must have fewer persons taken or captured.

3. **Kiddyadi** is a rude form of the base-ball play of the Americans and is somewhat similar to the primitive form of cricket. The materials used are a club like a ruler called *Kiddy* and a short stick called *Pullu.* A hole is dug; the side which hits-out stands by it and hits the *Pullu* out into the field. If the *Pullu* is caught the hitter is *out.* If the *pullu* is fielded it is aimed at the hole which has to be guarded by the

hitter with his *Kiddy*. If the *Pullu* falls within a *Kiddy* length of the hole or into the hole the hitter is *out*. This is continued until the whole side is out. There are several forms of this play.

4. **Kilittaddu** is a very popular game because of the little space required for it and because it keeps every person occupied. The play ground is levelled and divided into squares so that they may form into rows of squares. The number of squares depends upon the number of persons playing. The squares are thus arranged.

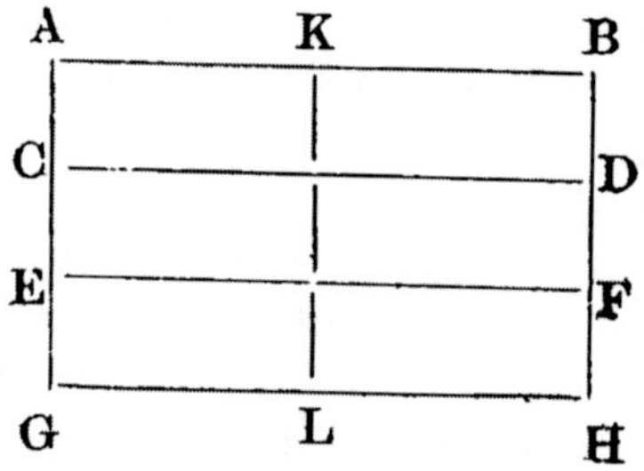

The ground above indicated is enough for eight players four on each side. The side that takes the offensive remains in front of the Court. The defensive side arranges its men as follows. Three men are put on each of the lines C D, E F and G H. The fourth man the leader or Captain may be anywhere on the boundary lines or on K L. The offensive side gets in from the side between A and B. They try to get out on the side between G and H without going beyond A G and B H and without being touched by any of the three men while in the very act of crossing the lines and by the captain from his lines. The captain may touch the opposing men jumping from one corner to another taking care not to step inside the lines. Any one of them getting so touched, or going out of the side lines makes his side "out" so that they have to take the position for the defence. If any one of the men have managed to come out between G and H he tries to return in a similar way between A and B. In so doing he must be careful not to get into the square where the man who tries to get out of G H may be standing. If he or any others who may follow him, successfully comes out of the line between A and B the whole side wins, and they get in as before the other side continuing still to be on the defensive.

In some places there are slight modifications in the rules, the increasing of the squares is always done by pairs towards G H.

Kenthy is also a popular game. A circle is drawn on the ground. One side gets into the circle. One man from the other side gets into the circle hopping on one leg, the other leg never touching the ground, for then he will be *out*. He may also get *out* by getting out of the circle. He tries to touch any one or more of the other side. Those who are touched and those who get out of the circle are counted *out*. So that there would be men getting *out* on both the sides. The winners are those who have less men out.

Koladdam is a very interesting game and requires a great deal of practice. It is mostly taught in vernacular schools. To the top of a pole are attached as many strings as there are boys engaged in the game. Each boy takes hold of the end of each of the strings in one hand and a short stick in the other. They sing a song to a certain tune keeping time by striking at his neighbour's stick. In so doing they move from place to place and the strings are interwoven to a design. Then with the same music the strings are separated. Another song and another design is now tried.

Ammanai is a game of having many balls in the hand and throwing them up in succession and catching them in turn. One person alone does it. The others take their turn. This is an ancient game mentioned in the Mahabharta.

Panthadikirathu is a game like base-ball among the Americans. The ball used is as soft as a tennis ball; the club used is something like a cricket bat but very thin and light. Bases are marked as in base ball. The game proceeds like base-ball but a person is *out* when the ball is aimed at the person making the rounds while he is between the bases. Girls delight in this game. This is another ancient game mentioned in the Mahabarata.

Chinky. Men sit round in a circle facing the centre. A cloth is twisted, carried round by one of the players and dropped. The person behind whom it is dropped should take it up and chase the one who dropped it. He (former) may beat him with it until he (latter) takes the seat. If he fails to take up the cloth dropped he is beaten with it by the person who dropped it. The game continues.

Pasuvum Pulium. (Cow and Tiger) is a game which consists of a number of persons standing round with their hands clasped guarding one inside who represents the cow while another who represents the tiger tries to force his way into the enclosure and carry away his prize. The "tiger" wins by merely touching the "cow."

Among the minor games may be mentioned·

Mankoddai Podukiratu a game with a mango nut.

Kanpottukiratu, Hide and seek.

Illuppai koddai Kaddukiratu, a game with Iluppai seeds.

Cocoanut Fighting; The game of breaking the opponent's cocoanut with his own.

The games of cricket, foot ball under the association rules and lawn tennis are now becoming popular among the school boys; so are sports such as jumps, races, vaulting, leap-frog &c.

INDOOR GAMES.

The chief of the indoor games are the following:

Chess,

Thayam, } Games with dice cards.
Chokkaddan, }

Pandi.

Dog and Tiger etc.

Map
OF THE
JAFFNA PENINSULA
Scale of 4 miles to an inch
Miles
THE ISLANDS
KARACHCHI
PUNAKARI
PACHCHILAI
JAFFNA